ALAN McGEE
& THE STORY OF
CREATION RECORDS

THIS ECSTASY ROMANCE CANNOT LAST

PAOLO HEWITT

MAINSTREAM
PUBLISHING

EDINBURGH AND LONDON

First published in Great Britain in 2000 by
MAINSTREAM PUBLISHING COMPANY (EDINBURGH) LTD
7 Albany Street
Edinburgh EH1 3UG

ISBN 1 84018 350 0

A catalogue record for this book is available from the British Library

Typset in Gill Sans and Neuland Black

Printed and bound in Great Britain by Creative Print and Design Wales

CONTENTS

ACKNOWLEDGEMENTS

Mighty big thanks to Alan McGee for all the help and honesty. Similar salutations to everyone else who sat down with me. I hope the book does your story some kind of justice. Truth be told, this book simply would not exist without the skill and professionalism of my tape transcription harem. Take a big bow, Debbie Hicks and Emily Fitzroy. You deserve it, the pair of you.

ALAN McGEE AND THE STORY OF CREATION RECORDS

FOREWORD

For 17 years Creation was my life.

Although I felt that it had come to an end a few years previously, I just couldn't admit it to myself that the label was finished. Moving on from people and situations is the hardest thing in life to do. To be honest, we should all have killed it off the minute Oasis walked offstage at Knebworth. It would have been amazing to be confirmed as having the biggest group in the world and to have split up the label on the spot. As it was I killed the label three years later. We were still really big but the point had been made: in 1996 the aesthetic between psychedelia and Punk rock was now the biggest thing in the world. It was a job done. Over and out.

After that we lost our way and the really promising groups like Trashmonk and Arnold couldn't get the sunlight they deserved because of the glare of a successful Creation. They also had to live with the prospect of never being another Oasis. Why did I leave? For a million reasons, but here's one example: I went to see Oasis at Wembley recently. I wasn't going to go as I feel that these big gigs are the opposite of rock 'n' roll. Though I was going to the home of English football, in my head I was going to catch early Oasis with the raw Primals at a great venue like Reading.

So I found myself on the Saturday night at the bar and I spot an ex-Creation employee who is now a Big Brother records employee. I give her a cuddle and she then tells me she cannot believe that me and my mate Ian Scouser – also an ex-Creation employee – have better seats than her. So I look at her and say 'Sorry . . . but I only discovered the group'.

It was a funny incident and it made me glad to be rid of most of the people that had displayed this kind of *überego* in the record industry. Later on she comes up to me and says, 'Have you got the needle with you?' I had, by now, forgotten all about it but I told her since she brought it up that this was typical of the kind of thing that made me start Poptones and leave Creation. They were all worrying about who had the best seats and where that put them in the hierarchy within the ever-growing corporate structure, when all they should have been worrying about was the label and the bands.

It's a question of the difference between the music business and people who love music. When I got rid of the lot of them and started Poptones I suddenly started to remember why I loved music.

This book is about that struggle. It is as funny as fuck, and what's more, it's all true.

Alan McGee,
Summer 2000

CAST OF CHARACTERS

ALAN McGEE — former head of Creation Records and founder of Poptones Records. (AM)

SUSAN McGEE — younger sister of Alan. Proud. (SM)

JOE FOSTER — co-founder of Creation Records, now director of music at Poptones. (JF)

ED BALL — ex-Creation Records all-rounder and now Poptones recording artist. (EB)

JEFF BARRETT — ex-Creation press officer, now head of Heavenly Records. (JB)

MARTIN KELLY — partner in Heavenly Records. (MK)

LAURENCE — ex-Creation press officer, now PR for various drum and bass luminaries. (L)

KLE — ex-PA to Alan McGee at Creation Records and now scriptwriter. (K)

TIM ABBOT — ex-Creation marketing man, now music business consultant. (TA)

CHRIS ABBOT — founder and head of Creation off-shoot label Infonet, now management consultant. (CA)

MARK GARDNER — ex-vocalist with Ride, now member of The Animal House. (MG)

KATE HOLMES — ex-Frazier Chorus, married Alan McGee in 1998. (KH)

SIMON STEPHENS — ex-Primal Scream co-manager and now estate agent to the stars. (SS)

INTRODUCTION

ED BALL: WHAT YEARS WERE YOU AT *NME*?
PAOLO HEWITT: I was there from 1983 to 1990.

EB: AT THE BEGINNING OF THAT PERIOD COULD YOU DESCRIBE SOME OF THE PEOPLE WHO WERE MASSIVE FANS OF CREATION?
PH: Danny Kelly was one, The Legend, who of course made a really bad record for Creation and then later on, James Brown.

EB: AND WHERE DID YOU FIRST MEET ALAN?
PH: The first time I met Alan was in 1988. Well, to understand all this you really have to skip back two years to when *NME* issued that C86 tape, proclaiming that all these Indie bands were the future of music. I thought they were mad. For me, that music meant absolutely nothing. It was so sub standard. At that time I was just checking loads of hip hop and contemporary soul and getting really excited about it and along with a few other writers trying to point out that this was the music that *NME* should be championing. Anyway, one day I said to Danny Kelly, look give me this C86 tape. I did so because I figured they were so excited about this tape that there had to be something going on. I didn't even get to the fifth track. You know, I grew up on The Beatles and great pop and soul and I know good music and this was just poor. I put Creation into the Indie label slot and left well alone. Then Acid House happened. I was one of the first writers to cover it and soon enough, Acid House was the future and rock is dead for good. I used to go to a club in Dingwalls called High on Hope, which happened on a Thursday night. This is when I first met Alan. Alan came up to me and said, 'You're

ALAN McGEE AND THE STORY OF CREATION RECORDS

Paolo Hewitt and you're right about Acid House.' And he walked off. I was taken by that. This was *NME*'s fave geezer, the King of Indie rock, telling me that what I was saying was totally correct. I respected him for that.

EB: DID YOU NEVER THINK, GIVEN YOUR '60S THING, THAT SOMEONE WHO HAD A LABEL CALLED CREATION MIGHT BE INTO THE SAME THING AS YOU?
PH: I was judging it on the people who liked it. I've never been a great fan of that band and also the label never came up in discussion within my circle. It just never came up.

And as far as I was concerned Creation was on the other side, so I didn't take note of Creation because of the vibe I was getting from certain people.

EB: WHEN DID YOU MEET ALAN THE NEXT TIME?
PH: When I was writing my first Oasis book. I interviewed him at his flat in Baker Street. I thought he was candid, had a good slant on things and his interview was really valuable for my book. I liked him. He was open. He wasn't playing any games. He told me this funny story about when he was in the clinic and sometimes the people there would set off the alarm clock just to get out onto Baker Street and make a run for the nearest drug dealer. Anyway, he's standing outside feeling quite fragile when a girl comes up and says 'Oh there's my handbag,' picks up a crisp bag that is in the gutter and walks away. I think his words were, 'If she thought a crisp packet was her handbag, that's when I knew I didn't have too much to worry about.'

EB: AND DID YOUR RELATIONSHIP DEVELOP FROM THERE?
PH: Not really. I saw him at a few Oasis gigs and we spoke but it was kind of chit-chat stuff. Then I saw him on that *Omnibus* documentary he did and I thought, 'Why are you in music and not football?' All he spoke about was Rangers and Chelsea.

EB: DID YOU EVER THINK AT THIS TIME THAT YOU WOULD BE WRITING A BOOK ABOUT ALAN AND HIS LABEL?

PH: No way. The reason it came about was this. I was right about rock in the '80s. It was rubbish. In the '90s things started to happen. Music really started to merge together. One example. Look at the Social club and what that achieved. It said listen to Barry White, listen to The Standells and ain't it a trip? That whole period was an inspiring time, a real loosening up of the barriers. Shaking off the '80s was the best thing you could do in the '90s. I miss those times now. Anyway, I was writing my book *The Soul Stylists*, when the phone rang. It was a girl at a book company who wanted to see me for a drink. She had an idea for a book which was a history of Creation. My first reaction to this was, there are three groups I dig – Oasis, Primal Scream and Teenage Fanclub – and what unites them? Creation Records.

But then we found out that there was another book being written so we backed off from there. I went back to working on *The Soul Stylists*. January 2000 comes. Oasis are playing *The Jools Holland Show*. I go down there, bump into McGee and start talking. I tell him I was offered a book on him. He says do it. But there's another book being done I say. Now I don't know if McGee is a publicity junkie who loves the idea of having two books on him or if he genuinely felt that this other book was going to be so detailed it would miss the point. He was insistent that I write something. So I went over to interview him one afternoon in March. We spoke for about three hours and I thought I have got to do something with this stuff because it is really, really revealing, it's interesting and it feels honest. And I should say here that what I was attempting to do within this book was capture the *spirit* of Creation Records. That company put out an astounding amount of music and I had no interest in dissecting every piece of it. No interest at all. After that first McGee interview I just knew that this was a great story and that the best thing was to highlight the great albums and the artists whilst painting the overall picture. That's why I interviewed the people within the company and not the bands.

ALAN McGEE AND THE STORY OF CREATION RECORDS

EB: WERE YOU SURPRISED AT HOW DISARMING ALAN WAS?

PH: I was, and I started thinking that most of the people who have been in rehab that I have come into contact with, they come out and they can't stop talking. When they're taking drugs they don't say a word.

I've also noticed that when people who are doing drugs suddenly fall ill they never ever tell the doctors what they've been up to. Check Alan's interviews in this book. Every time he gets ill on a plane or in a hotel he won't tell the medical people he's taken something. It's like he's guilty about it because he knows himself that he's fucking up. If you get up and do a line first thing in the morning you're not going to tell anyone because the majority are bound to say, 'First thing in the morning? That's a bit strong.' And you're going to feel bad, not good. Unless of course you're with other drug fiends which is what McGee was doing. Maybe when you go into rehab, they teach you how to lose guilt so when you get out you can tell the world everything because it is no longer an issue and their criticisms can't hurt you. What do you think?

EB: I think you're absolutely right about the guilt thing. I'm not so sure it's the therapy because I think Alan has always been open. He would be open about his private life, his home life. I'm naturally a more guarded person and I would be shocked, as a lot of people are, by the things he would say.

PH: Yeah, the way he talks about his relationship with Bobby and all the other people in the book. And I love the way he remembers things to do with drugs. Like when he's on three E at The Hacienda and he goes up to Shaun Ryder who gives him half a pill which actually knocks him to the furthermost parts of the cosmos but at the time he's thinking, half a pill? You tight bastard! Details like that made me laugh. Talking to him and then discovering loads of things in common. His passion for The Jam and Dexy's, his view that Paul Weller and Kevin Rowland were probably the only two musicians in the early to mid '80s worth bothering with.

EB: That reminds me of something you said. You said Alan seems to create friendships very easily but the first hint of disloyalty or trouble, bang, he is off.

PH: I think it's because he is so passionate about something that the first hint of trouble, he's off. Also, going on the evidence, he's been right to back off in a lot of cases.

EB: DO YOU FEEL THAT YOU'VE BECOME A CONFESSOR FIGURE IN ALL THIS? LIKE A CATHOLIC PRIEST WHO HAS LISTENED TO ALL THESE PEOPLE?

PH: He said that to me the other day. He said someone wanted to interview him but he had to blow it out and he was glad because my book had exhausted him. I really like this book a lot because without any intent on my part it has developed a real novel-like structure to it. You start with this invisible guy in Scotland who has his life turned round by Punk rock and starts getting ambitious. Then you see the relationship he has with Bobby, his best mate, and then all these colourful characters suddenly start appearing in his life. He gets on the rollercoaster and it throws him all over the world.

If you wrote this book as fiction I doubt if people would believe it. But here it is, in glorious black and white.

EB: WHAT DO YOU THINK ALAN GETS FROM IT?

PH: He gets close to the magic. And he's fatally attracted to obsessives.

EB: DID YOU DISCOVER ANY MUSIC IN WRITING THIS BOOK?

PH: Two albums stood out for me. The first My Bloody Valentine album and the Trashmonk album.

EB: Music you might have missed otherwise.

PH: Ten years ago if you had told me I would have been writing this book I really would have laughed you off the dancefloor. Now, well, it's been a great journey for me, a trip into something I was unaware of but which I'm so glad I was open enough to explore. My only regret is that back in 1988 you lot didn't get on the blower and invite me to one of your Westgate Street parties. I must say that was *awfully* rude of you, don't you think?

IN THE BEGINNING

The '80s, it was horrible. There was very little to get really excited about but Alan actually fought his corner. He wasn't doing it out of charity, he was saying, 'No, this is what I want to do and I'm going to fucking do it.' He went to the brink on many many occasions and he still did not give up, and for that I give him ultimate respect. He taught me all that. I really respect him. He never ever did it solely for the money. It wasn't a crusade. It was just this guy going, 'I've worked for British Rail, I've lived in this town long enough, I've got a shot here and I'm gonna go for it.' And that boy did.

Jeff Barrett,
Heavenly Records, 2000

SUSAN McGEE

PAOLO HEWITT: IS ALL YOUR FAMILY LIKE YOU? IS YOUR DAD LIKE YOU?

SUSAN McGEE: No.

PH: Or your mum, is she . . . ?

SM: My mum was definitely the brains between my mum and dad. She was the one that was the driving force kind of thing, you know, very much more the dominant parent. I never really seen my dad or had a relationship with my dad up to a couple of years ago really. It's kind of weird. Because he was always working and he had a job at night as well and like he was always just this guy that was always busy. Do you know what I mean? So my mum was a main focus.

PH: HOW OLD WERE YOU WHEN YOUR MUM DIED?

SM: I was 21.

PH: You were 21. Was that a real big . . .

SM: No. I blocked it out with drugs and just kind of got my head around it about two years ago. It was a weird one really. Couldn't talk about it up to about two years ago.

PH: And what about Alan? How did he take it?

SM: He's the same. It was only recently that he's really kind of got his head around the whole thing, you know.

ALAN McGEE

ALAN McGEE: I went to Kings Park Secondary School. I left school – unofficially 1975 – but officially I left school in 1977. I was 16-and-a-half. I got one O level. And I was mates – I wasn't big mates – with Bobby Gillespie. We'd started going to concerts. And punk came along. Bob wasn't as fast up on Punk as I was. By April 1977, I was bang into Punk. I remember when 'God Save the Queen' came out at the same time as 'Go Buddy Go' and 'Sheena Is A Punk Rocker'. And I remember going out and buying three Punk singles dressed in, believe it or not, a fucking Adidas kagoul. Fucking fashion comes around right? I remember walking down the street thinking I have bought into the revolution and at that point, I must admit, I think my life totally changed. I went from being like a suburban kid to jumping over to the other side of the fence, even though nobody around me probably would ever have noticed the difference.

When I left school, I got a job in a factory for £17 a week. It was absolutely shit. You won't believe this but I was making shirt collars. For £17 I used to put these things in a machine and pull a lever for eight hours a day. I did it for three weeks then I chucked it and I was on the dole for about a month. I then got a job on a building site for six months. I was an apprentice electrician. And it was just fucking rotten. But what was great was you had the radio on and there was everything from The Jam to things like 'Looking After Number One' by the Boomtown Rats and 'Complete Control' by The Clash. That was Radio One. It was the kind of poppy end of Punk but it was great because you could sit and you could listen to the radio and it was alright. And then

I bought my first guitar. I wanted to be in a Punk band that I could be able to *play* in. Around the end of 1977 I used to listen to this show called the Brian Ford . . . fucking, what was it, Brian Ford's *Punk Rock Wednesday* show . . . I can't remember what the fuck it was called! It was the Punk show on Radio Clyde and it was every Wednesday night. And so, basically, right, I was just bang into it and I heard this advert and it was for a band called The Drains, and this is how I met Andrew Innes (Primal Scream band member). The Drains needed a bass player. It was Innes on lead guitar and this toff guy called Pete Buchanan on drums. He was Innes' next-door neighbour and he went to a private school. Since I was the only applicant I joined the band. Pete Buchanan? We kicked him out after about, I dunno, two or three months because he was a twat. And it was me and Innes, the start of me and Innes, playing in bands. I was mates with Bobby and he used to come up on a Friday, and me, Innes and Bob had these imaginary bands called like . . .

PAOLO HEWITT: DID INNES KNOW BOBBY?
AM: No, no. He met Bobby through me right. Bob liked Innes. He did take a shine to him because Innes could play the Punk anthems and stuff like that. We used to *do* the whole Clash album. Me and Innes drinking beer and Gillespie – I don't think Gillespie drank at that time – would roll about the ground being like Iggy Pop meets Jimmy Pursey. I think Bob liked Sham around that time. Innes was into The Jam before me. He saw them at Shuffles. I think they played there in '77. And then by like late '77 I saw The Jam in the Apollo. So me and Innes were into it but Bob thought that Weller was a Tory because he said that thing about vote Conservative. Bob's dad was a Trade Unionist so anything like that was a touchy subject. I remember being in Glasgow Central Station talking with Bob and saying, 'The Jam are a good band', and he was really going mental. But by the end of the 'Modern World' tour Gillespie was bang into The Jam. He'd come around to it, do you know what I mean? Then me and Innes went off and we were in some terrible bands together.

We were in this band H_2O which had two fucking hit singles and the guy went on to *Top of the Pops* with a Yo-Yo, 20 years before Yo-Yos were fucking famous. We were in that group four or five months. We left that. And then we formed this band Newspeak with the guitarist out of Lloyd Cole and the Commotions, Neil Clark. And so we were in that band for a bit. Then we left Glasgow. I didn't want to go. I had just finally got a girlfriend. It is kind of like, still in my head today that if Innes hadn't made me come to London, I would never have had Creation. So when Innes went, 'We'll never make it in Glasgow, we've got to come to London' he was so right. So it was me, Innes and this guy Jack Riley and we moved in initially to this bedsit in like Tooting.

PH: DO YOU REMEMBER THE ADDRESS?

AM: Innes might remember it. But Tooting is where we were. Basically, me and Innes – and we were particularly cruel in those days, we were like nasty kind of characters. We weren't really cool but were like vitriolic little guys. And Jack Riley was this sort of playboy character. He was the singer in Newspeak so he was the one who got to shag the women. So, the bottom line is we'd taken Jack away from his kind of comfort blanket which was loads of women shagging him, to living in this fucking expensive place with these two cheeky little guys. So Jack couldn't hack it and he went back. Me and Innes ended up moving into a squat. We lived in and out of this squat. Sometimes I would live in it, sometimes Innes would live in it. And the only good thing that really came out of that period was that we formed the Laughing Apple.

Now up to that point, I'll be honest with you, I knew nothing about drugs right. Which sounds unbelievable for a 19-year-old kid that's moved to London. But I knew nothing about drugs. Drugs in Glasgow, they never really were fucking happening in my scene and Gillespie didn't take drugs. Innes never took drugs. We never really took drugs. I think maybe I'd done speed once or something but I'd hardly done any drugs. And we got this drummer called Mark. I can't remember his second name. We met him through this pink-haired woman called Karen. Innes would remember her. He's probably still in contact with her. And she was part Punk beauty, part *Rocky Horror Show*. It was one of them. It was like it could go either way. One day you would wake up, see her and go, 'Fuck, I'd really like to fuck you,' and another day you'd wake up and you'd go, 'Fucking hell man, it's the Addams Family'! It went like that. I never slept with her, but basically she got us this drummer Mark. And it was in the back of this squat where me and Innes ended up living over the next six months.

PH: Whereabouts was the squat?

AM: St. Alphonsus Road in Clapham.

PH: Saint . . . ?

AM: St. Alphonsus Road. And it's all been gentrified now. And I think all the houses there are now worth about £700,000, but then it was just a row of empty houses, and it was all full of people that had jumped the Italian army, jumped the English army. And they were all smack heads. And they had all gravitated towards this area. I remember seeing some guy light up the spoon, get the school tie, and bang it up. And until he got the school tie out and he got the fucking needle out I didn't know what he was fucking doing. And then I was like, I'd seen it on TV and I went, 'Fuck, this is heroin!' And he went, 'Do you want any?' And me and Innes were like, 'No, we're alright,' you know what I mean? And then seeing what the smack did to all these people. They were always getting really fucking ill, you know, and they were really nice kids that were living there, but they were just so fucking run down. So that was kind of how I ended up not wanting to be part of, you know, the heroin sort of thing. And that really trailed on for the rest of my life.

PH: Let's talk a little bit about the music.

AM: We auditioned. Me and Innes auditioned the singer in The Chords, Billy. We had him right sussed; we weren't Mods. We were always Punk Rockers. I remember Noel Gallagher. I went to see Noel around *Morning Glory* time and he was hanging out and saying, 'Creation's a Mod label'. 'It's not a Mod label Noel, it's a Punk rock label'. And he said 'But you're not a Punk rocker McGee'. And I went, 'You don't understand. It's like where I'm coming from is Punk rock'. See, I might be clean and have my trousers all kind of Mod, right, but at the end of the day, the thing that turns my head more than Socialism or religion or drugs or anything is Punk. Do you know what I mean?

PH: HOW WERE YOU SURVIVING IN LONDON? HOW WERE YOU GETTING MONEY?
AM: I came down and I was on the dole. And then, I went and got a job for British Rail because I'd been working for British Rail in Glasgow and I, basically, persuaded them to give me another job. I started at Paddington. I was some sort of clerk. It was a really typical '70s thing. There used to be these jobs, right, and nobody understood what these jobs were. I used to have these papers that I would have to move out of my 'in' tray into my 'out' tray. I couldn't ever make head nor tail of what I was actually really doing. It wasn't really obvious. It was really oblique how you fitted into it. And then unbelievably, I ended up getting a promotion to fucking Shenfield British Rail station. I was like 19 years old and I got promoted to a CO3 which meant I was suddenly responsible for all the wages at Shenfield train station. And all I wanted to be was the bass player in The Laughing Apple and be a pop star.
PH: So what year did you say you started with British Rail in Glasgow?
AM: 1979. And then I chucked it.

PH: WHEN DID YOU COME TO LONDON?
AM: June 1980.

PH: WHEN DO YOU REJOIN BRITISH RAIL?
AM: Probably about August.
PH: 1980?
AM: Yeah. Cos I realised that because I had good references I could get another job, so I got a job. I started, I ended up in Shenfield as a CO3.
PH: Where the fuck is Shenfield?
AM: Essex somewhere. An hour out of London. And I was travelling to Clapham North, living in this bedsit.

PH: WHEREABOUTS WAS INNES AT THIS TIME?

AM: He lived in a bedsit in Wandsworth. And he wrote this song at the time called, 'Wandsworth Common Northside' which was . . . actually I can still sing you the tune. It was quite a good song.

Then he ended up descending into drugs hell, you know, he ended up in this squat with the fucking army guys, ended up with fucking hepatitis and going home for nine months.

PH: Right. And that leaves you on your own in London. On British Rail. Did you have any other friends or . . .

AM: Well, to be honest, Paolo, I never really made good friends until I started running the Living Room Club. Kind of '82 or '83. I knew people though . . . Dick Green who then went on to do Creation with me, he was friends with Ken Popple, the Laughing Apple drummer. And we brought him in as the second guitar player when Innes went home. Innes went home for nine months and Dick became the guitar player. And that was The Laughing Apple. We did one single but it was a really terrible version of Joy Division. I don't know if you've ever heard it. It is absolutely like one of these things that you hope people will never hear. And then the band broke up. But we all stayed sort of pals.

PH: So who's in the band when you broke up? You, Dick Green . . .

AM: Me, Dick Green, Ken and this boy from Newcastle who had joined them as the second guitarist because like Dick had become the first guitar player.

PH: HOW WAS INNES DOING?

AM: Andrew wasn't well. One of his kidneys doesn't work because of hepatitis. So he's on one kidney now. That's why when Innes was caning it in the early '90s it was incredibly dangerous for him because I mean if that kidney had went Innes was gone. So then I tried to chuck music. And that was about '81 or '82.

PH: You what, sorry?

AM: I tried to chuck music.

PH: Chuck it?

AM: Aye. Cos it all came to a head. The group wasn't doing anything.

We'd just done this tour with Eyeless in Gaza and somebody nicked my Yamaha bass guitar which, at the time, was worth £400. Eyeless in Gaza must have taken it out and put it in the van because some Edinburgh ned went up and smacked the guy in the throat and ran away with my guitar right. Then the police at the time made a really fucking cack-handed effort to get it back – you know, guy looks big so we'll run the other way. Then on the way back Dick hits some black ice and nearly totalled the van. And my wife at the time, Yvonne, got thrown out through the windscreen right and got whiplash for, like two weeks after it. It wrote the van off. And unbelievably we all came out of it unscathed. I don't know if you've ever been in or had a car accident. It's like being in a tumble dryer. What was scary was that afterwards there were jugger-nauts fucking hitting black ice and sliding off the same stretch of road.

PH: Whereabouts was this?

AM: This was between Edinburgh and Glasgow. I remember going in to see Gillespie the next day right and saying, 'We wrote the van off and nearly got killed' and – this is pure Gillespie – he started laughing. I snapped, 'I nearly died you little cunt, right'. But he wasn't even trying to be funny. I think, when Bob doesn't know what to say, he laughs. I mean he's probably got better as he's got older but essentially I don't think he could deal with the fact that I'd come out and said, 'We nearly got killed. The van got written off.' And all he could do was laugh which is kind of like bizarre. It was good, though, because it made me realise that if I was going to be involved seriously in music it was not in a band. I mean, some people go on to be 42 right and they're still going, 'I could be a pop star'. And it's like if you haven't made it by then you ain't ever going to fucking do it. And so I had come to that conclusion pretty early. So then I tried to get music out of my system. Not like stop listening to music. I was still obsessed with listening to music. But I thought that I'd fucking better knuckle down.

PH: IF SOMEBODY SAID TO YOU, 'WHAT WAS THE MUSIC OF THE LAUGHING APPLE LIKE?' WHAT WOULD YOU SAY?

AM: It was . . . I suppose it was Indie, but it was influenced by the '60s.

PH: WHERE DID THE NAME COME FROM?

AM: It was influenced a bit by The Jam as well because Innes really loved them. I think maybe there might be a book called *The Laughing Apple*. But I don't think . . . I think if we're famous for anything it was when we supported The Scars at the Moonlight Club. Me and Innes had a record player. We did four songs, jumped off the stage, put The Cure's 'Jumping Someone Else's Train' on, danced in the audience, then ran back up on stage and played another four songs. It was a fucking bizarre band!

PH: Were there many other things you did like that?

AM: I'll remember as we go on. I started promoting gigs at this musicians' collective in Gloucester Avenue called Communication Club. And I put on The TV Personalities, The Go-Betweens. Tony Fletcher was the first person I booked. I booked his band called The Apocalypse. I lost money every single night. Every single night we put something on we lost money. And I just thought, 'I'm a terrible business man. I lose money at all these things.' I was earning £70 a week as a British Railway clerk and I was losing £70 to £100 a week.

PH: You put your own money into it?

AM: Yeah, yeah, yeah. So I was losing money doing it. So I just thought, I'm rubbish at this. So after about two months I just stopped it for about another year. But around the time before I started again, Tony Fletcher wrote this incredible thing in an article. You've got to remember this was the time of Kajagoogoo and fucking Dead or Alive and all that rubbish right. Fletcher's bottom line was, 'Don't sit on your ass, you're a Punk Rocker, form a club, form a band, write a magazine, make a film, whatever you do fucking do something with your fucking life'.

And I fucking totally identified with that. So I went and started again. I did my magazine *Communication Blur* which only sold about 500 copies but it was great fun doing it. Then I started the Living Room. The first night something happened. There had been a sea change. I don't know what the fuck it was. It was June 1983. Or May 1983. We put on The Nightingales. And 200 or 300 people showed up in this room, Paolo, I'm not taking the piss, about double the size of this kitchen right. It was in a *room* above a pub.

PH: This is Gloucester Avenue?

AM: No this was now Adam's Arms, Conway Street. And the reason it was called the Living Room was because it *was* a big living room! It was a bit bigger than this. It wasn't much bigger. But I rammed, believe it or not, about 300 people in it. No security. Me and Dick and Joe Foster on the door. Everybody just around the band. And the band playing in the fireplace.

PH: You just mentioned Joe Foster. But how does he come into it?

AM: He comes into it because me and Dick started it initially, then Joe came on board to help us do it.

PH: Do the Collective?

AM: Yeah. I'd booked The TV Personalities. And I had always heard of this guy Joe from Hendon. I knew that Dan Tracey had been making a record with Joe from Hendon and his band. And I walked into the club and the first thing Joe Foster said to me was, 'You owe me £6'. And I went 'Who the fuck are you?' And he goes, 'I'm Joe from Hendon.' I think he said, 'I had to fork out for a fucking taxi and you owe me'. Totally lost out on aggression. And I was like, 'Alright, here's your money'. Do you know what I mean? I don't even know if I gave him it. I think I said, 'I'll pay you when I pay you,' blah, blah, blah, you know. And that was how I met Joe. But we became really close within the next month.

PH: That quickly yeah?

AM: Yeah, really fast.

PH: Why? What did you have between you?

AM: Just music. Just Punk. Just attitude. He definitely shaped the way that I thought about music. I was into Punk and I was into, you know, a lot of fucking things. But he got me into the Velvets and stuff like that, which was obviously pretty important because of the Mary Chain and everything. And we just became pals. But what happened was there had been a big change. Whereas a year before what I was doing was sort of inventing Indie rock. I just didn't know that I was inventing it. I was putting on all these bands and nobody was coming. Like 50 people would come and see a band as good as The Go-Betweens and 30 people would come and see The TV Personalities. Then a year later 250 people were coming to see The TV Personalities and suddenly it was as if I was the only promoter in London that had sussed out that these bands were actually popular. Something had happened and suddenly there was an Indie audience whereas there hadn't been one before. These people weren't even releasing records. And the John Curds [promoter] all these kind of people weren't putting these people on. So I was the only game in town. I ended up putting two or three gigs on a week.

PH: DO YOU THINK THAT YOUR SUCCESS WAS PART OF A REACTION TO THE CHART MUSIC OF THE TIME? WHAM, SPANDAU BALLET AND ALL THAT?

AM: Totally. That's what it was. But when we were doing it, because I was young, I never realised that's what it was. But now you think back to what it was, it was definitely that. And that's how I ended up having tons of pals. And that's how I broke through the media really fast as well. Because if you're on the door at a club that everybody wants to get into, you meet loads of people. I was putting the gigs on so kids were saying 'geezer' and all that stuff.

I'd started putting out records. By about January 1984 I'd put out Pastels records and Jasmine Mink's records, and the journalists at that point were all coming along so I was getting loads of publicity. And it was the best PR exercise I'd ever done really. So basically that's how we met all these people like Danny Kelly and Everett True.

PH: The Legend.

AM: I knew The Legend before that but there was a guy called Neil Taylor, he knew us and there were others, so to be honest, right, even if it wasn't a good night the club always got good reviews even if the bands didn't. So we built this thing. By the time that we started putting out our own records, the journalists owed us so many fucking favours.

PH: There was always that kind of groundswell support for you. See, what I found when I joined NME was that all those writers you're talking about hated the fact that they missed Punk and they were always trying to relive it.

AM: I never saw it like that but you might be actually right.

PH: That's what it was. I used to think, 'You missed it, you can't re-invent it with these groups'.

AM: I thought they were trying to re-invent sort of Rough Trade 1979 or something. That's what I thought.

PH: No it was just Punk that they wanted. But, of course, none of those bands had a Johnny Rotten.

AM: Completely. And the only band that stood the test of time was Primal Scream, you know. All the other bands never lasted.

PH: So anyway, so you're doing this club and it's getting really popular.

AM: And so then we started doing the records but of course, nobody would play them on the radio and then . . .

PH: HOW DID YOU START DOING THE RECORDS?

AM: Well, we were making money.

PH: Were you still at British Rail?

AM: Yes I'm still at British Rail but I chucked it by about the end of '84 or something like that. No, end of '83. I was making money. I was earning £70 a week as a British Rail clerk and £500 a week as a promoter. I had a few champagne parties. I don't even think it was champagne in those days but, I mean, I'd go out and get pissed and have ten beers. And I had money and Joe had money. Me and Joe were on the piss, and then we just went 'Fuck, we've got to start a label'. We started Creation.

PH: When was that?

AM: Well we put out a Legend record that was one of the worst records we've ever put out. That was June 1983. And we never did anything else, apart from a couple of flexi-discs.

PH: Sorry, how did you go about doing it though?

AM: Well, first I started a label called Autonomy which was through The Laughing Apple. So I knew how to record a record, take it to a, you know, guy that would press it and master it and then get bags and Bobby Gillespie would do the sleeves and all that sort of stuff.

PH: HOW MANY RECORDS DID YOU DO WITH THE LAUGHING APPLE THEN?

AM: Three singles. Three 7-inch singles.

PH: So you learned through that process. And when did you start Autonomy?

AM: That was June 1980.

PH: And did you approach any record companies with The Laughing Apple?

AM: Yeah. Yeah well we never went to them, we never got in the door. We usually sent them tapes.

PH: And they would just ignore them?

AM: 'Fuck off'. Basically ignored us.

PH: So that made you decide, 'Fuck it, we're Punks, we're gonna do our own thing.'

AM: If you start off with low expectations you can be successful. It's the exact opposite of Liam Gallagher right, cos if Liam Gallagher never sells records he's got a huge problem with his life because he doesn't understand what I understand and what you understand and what loads of other people understand, that is about how it's all built up over a period, do you know what I mean? I went into pop music thinking that you sell seven million records and it would be like The Beatles and there's women outside the house, and all the things. And then you put these records out and you sell 700. But it actually doesn't matter. Because John Peel plays your record and it's you that's on the radio and you've done it. And it's fucking amazing, do you know what I mean? So my expectation of pop music went from thinking you'll sell seven million to thinking you'll sell 700.

So that was great. I mean it sounds terrible but it was actually really good for me because it was like that's where expectations started. I was saying before the phone rang, you've got to build it up over a period. So when we started a label we thought, 'We'll sell a thousand' of a thing. There was no big expectation, there was no fucking big heavy stuff going on. It was like, out of the first ten singles, only one of them ever sold over a thousand, and it was The Loft. And then the twelfth release that we put out was 'Upside Down' by The Jesus and Mary Chain.

PH: WHEN DID YOU MEET THEM?

AM: Well, how we met them was that Bobby Gillespie . . .

PH: Actually, before that, just give us a few of the singles you put out.

AM: I think one was The Legend, '73 and '83. Second was The Revolving Paint Dream with 'Flowers In The Sky'. Number three was Biff Bang Pow, '50 Years Of Fun'. The fourth was The Jasmine Minks. The fifth was The Pastels 'Something's Going On'. The sixth was The X-Men 'Do the Ghost'. The seventh was Biff Bang Pow 'There Must Be A Better Life'. The eighth was 'Where the Traffic Goes' by The Jasmine Minks. The ninth was The Loft. And the tenth was 'Destroys The Blues' by The Legend. The eleventh was The Pastels 'Million Tears'. And the twelfth was The Jesus and Mary Chain. That's how much I loved the label at that point cos today I can't even tell you the names of the things we released last year.

PH: Those ten, eleven singles, how were they perceived?

AM: Good reviews. Lost money on every single. So the label was probably down £4,000. But, you know, cos we were making these singles for £200 or £100. We were making these singles for fucking nothing.

PH: WERE YOU STILL RUNNING THE CLUB?

AM: Yeah, yeah, yeah.

PH: So you're running the club and the club is basically paying for the singles?

AM: That's how we were funding things, that's how we were funding the label, you know?

PH: It was you, Joe Foster and Dick. And you're going out and you're seeing bands and . . .

AM: Yeah, we are just living it. And we were just kids. We were like 24-year-old kids. And just totally into music. And I was living in Seven Sisters Road with Yvonne. I was married. And, you know, Joe was living with Ingrid who was the drummer in The Raincoats. And Dick was living with Elaine who he still lives with to this day. And we were just kids really. Just having a good time.

SUSAN McGEE

PAOLO HEWITT: KINGS PARK. THAT'S WHERE ALAN WENT TO SCHOOL WASN'T IT?

SUSAN McGEE: Nobody even noticed Alan. He used to go to school with his duffel coat on and just kind of come back, do you know what I mean? Nothing. I mean mostly what I remember from Alan's school days was like in his bedroom he had like 'God Save The Queen' posters up and 'Sheena Is A Punk Rocker'. He had me at like six years of age jumping up and down and off the beds to that. He was always right into it. I mean in the school days he was the one that had – I mean you could tell he was going to be rebellious – a temper on him that was unbelievable. Total fiery redhead. And every Sunday there would be a massive family feud because Alan kind of had no future at that time, do you know what I mean, just the usual. Bobby Gillespie would just come in and just sit down and snigger because they were all fighting and Alan was in the middle of it all. He would just sit in the corner and laugh. And my Gran would try and hit Bobby over the head with a tea towel. Hilarious. I remember one of my sisters getting married and three weeks before it, I got a skinhead cut and my mum went mental. And she said, 'Right. That's it. No way. I'm keeping you indoors. Nobody's seeing you like that'. And ten minutes later the doorbell rang and it was Alan and Bobby and the two of them turned around and went, 'Brilliant haircut. You should go for it tomorrow and get more off'. So I had to be a bridesmaid with a skinhead. And a tiara on. Lovely.

PH: WAS BOBBY ALAN'S CLOSEST FRIEND?

SM: Aye, I would say so, yeah.

PH: And what brought them together, music?

SM: It definitely must have been. And they lived pretty kind of near by, you know. Aye. And Colin Dobbins was the other close pal.

PH: Who was?

SM: Colin Dobbins. Hilarious.

PH: What was he like?

SM: Just one of these wee individuals. Just a kind of mad guy like, bizarre, just kind of a misfit almost. And every time he would come into the house he would have dogshit on his feet. Right up the stairs. Unreal. Honestly. Pretty accident prone I think, definitely. Might be lucky, you never know, some people class that as good luck don't they.

PH: So Kings Park? What's it like? I mean obviously I don't know.

SM: It's kind of pretty. That's where we are trying to move back to actually.

PH: Right. Is it like a working class sort of area?

SM: Aye working class but pretty quiet and quite residential. And the schools are still okay, they're not mental schools yet, so that's why we're trying to get back to there.

PH: And so, Alan always says he was completely nondescript but when Punk happened did he change his appearance?

SM: Well no. There wasn't much you could do with short curly ginger hair. You know what I mean.

PH: DO YOU REMEMBER THE GROUPS THAT ALAN LIKED?

SM: Buzzcocks. Sex Pistols. The Ramones. He did an audition over the phone for The Revillos.

PH: Did he. An audition?

SM: Aye. Bass guitar.

PH: How did he do that?

SM: Up in my mum and dad's bedroom. Just had the guitar plugged in. He had the phone sitting there and he auditioned over the phone for them.

PH: How did that come about? Did they advertise?

SM: It was in the *Melody Maker* or *NME*, aye.

PH: So he rang them up and said, 'listen'?

SM: Aye. Totally. So that was before he was even 18. He used to run away all the time as well. And book himself into hotels down in Shawlands which was ten minutes away. Have big fights with my mum and dad and storm out and say, 'That's it, I'm leaving this time'. He got his first flat when he was about 18 and it was a wee flat in the West End of Glasgow. And my mum and dad went to see what it was like and just came back saying it was worse than *Rising Damp*. That was a great start in life.

PH: WHY DID ALAN AND YOUR MUM AND DAD CLASH SO MUCH?

SM: I think the ideas they had of what they wanted their son to do was not anything like his, because he was so interested in the music thing.

PH: DID YOUR SISTER LAURA CONFORM THOUGH?

SM: Not really. Well to a point. I think she was kind of different. She was kind of more into art and she was into the art school thing on a Saturday and did stuff like that. She had a pal in the worst part of Glasgow, the Gorbals, but she never let on to my mum and dad because she knew that they would go mental. She used to disappear for weekends and that was to the Gorbals.

PH: So she was a bit of a rebel as well then?

SM: I know. In a way. A kind of quieter one.

PH: And what about yourself?

SM: Aye well, I moved out when I was about 18 and just kind of started kind of taking acid and doing all that kind of stuff. I had kind of conformed to the point where I was doing a secretarial job and all that and then I got to 21 and thought, 'Oh I'm not doing this any more. This is a no-no.' So I opened up my own shop and ran my own kind of business for three years and then ended up with £5,000 worth of debt to the Inland Revenue because everything was going down my throat or up my nose. That was mental.

PH: What shop was it, what did you have?

SM: It was a wee kind of designer club-wear shop. Biba Love it was called.

PH: So there is such a thing as a McGee entrepreneurial spirit?

SM: I think so aye. Well Alan definitely brought that out in me because when he moved away I was kind of the only one he would talk to, at first. I was only about 15 and I would sit on the phone to him. And he would be down in London, would be starting Creation and stuff and he'd say stuff like, 'Don't listen to mum and dad,' and 'You can do better than that,' and stuff like that. So that was always kind of in-built in my head that basically there's a big world out there and you can do whatever you want kind of thing.

PH: SO DO YOU THINK WITHOUT ALAN YOUR LIFE WOULD HAVE BEEN A BIT DIFFERENT?

SM: I think he was a stronger figure than my dad ever was anyway, do you know what I mean. I was much closer to my mum.

PH: It seems there are two things that have really struck me about all the people I have been talking to. One is that he does inspire a lot of people.

SM: Oh aye. He's definitely got a lot of drive in him. And I think that comes from the competition that my mum and dad put between Laura and Alan. They didn't do that with me because it was a bigger age gap. But between the two of them there was definitely like a kind of competitive streak going on.

PH: He said that. He said that the reason he did it all was to show his mum and his dad that he could do something. That okay, he wasn't going to be Muhammad Ali. He wasn't going to be Liam Gallagher. But he knew a good band when he saw one. And you'd agree with that as well?

SM: Oh aye. That was how it was. There's a lot of drive in him and he's constant, the energy in him is pretty high, you know.

CHAPTER ONE

ALAN McGEE

ED BALL: The first time I met Alan was at a club. It must have been the Living Room. I'd been forewarned because before that I'd been in this group, The TV Personalities with Joe Foster and Dan Tracey. Dan had said, 'Watch out, there's this guy around at the moment and he's just incredibly pushy, he's very charming and you won't know what's hit you when you meet him'. And I thought, 'Oh yeah!' This was '84. We'd been making records for seven years because we had started in 1977 and when you get to about 23 or 24 years of age, you think, nothing impresses me now. But I met Alan and I couldn't believe his enthusiasm. I actually thought, 'He's taking the piss'. He said, 'Your LP, This is London, is a fucking genius album, it's brilliant. You should do that song, 'If Only', as a single. You should do it with me and we'll rope in all the other guys, we'll get Bobby to do something on it.' And I said, 'Yeah, yeah, yeah, alright then'. So that would have been the first time I met him.

JOE FOSTER: Yeah, I was in The TV Personalities which started because of Punk and I played guitar and sometimes played bass, it depended. It was Ed Ball and a guy called Dan Tracey who were in the band, he was the lead singer. And Ed and I would do different things depending on who was around, who was in the band, what was going on.

Sometimes we were a three-piece, sometimes we were a five piece, it depended who we really had, how much money we had. We did one of the first kind of Indie singles, 'Part-Time Punks', that was quite big.

It sold a lot of records, it wasn't a hit. You didn't get hits in those days, you just did other stuff. Three or four albums and that was that. I kind of dropped in and out as I was trying to be sensible and go to college and stuff. Early on Dan and Ed wrote most of the songs and I started writing stuff later on.

EB: We'd done one album as The TV Personalities called *And Don't the Kids Just Love It* with John Steed and Twiggy on the cover. Dan and I were taking it from The Beatles and The Kinks and obviously The Jam. Through The Jam, that's when we found out about The Creation. And this is how flash and how arrogant we were. We wanted to try and release The Creation's back catalogue. So there's these 20-year-old herberts ringing up and saying, 'Yeah, well, you know, we want to license this stuff off you'.

JF: We liked The Who. We liked the American bands, The Byrds and the Velvet Underground and obviously all the Punk bands. We were very in with The Clash and the Pistols and stuff. Ed was always a huge fan of The Jam and The Buzzcocks because we thought they were really quite impressive. Especially The Buzzcocks for the way they had these really bubble gummy songs and just put them across totally straight faced. I found that really admirable, it was like quite brave. We would veer off in different ways, do different things. Sometimes we'd do very kind of '60s-type pop, sometimes we'd do very funky things, sometimes we'd do quite odd avant-gardey type of things, it just depended how we felt really. The only time we stuck with something was when there was a kind of phoney psychedelic revival going on and all these people picked up on us and we thought, 'Alright, fair enough, we'll play that shit for a bit.' This was 1981 or 1982. It was quite good, we spent most of our time in Germany. We were kind of minor pop stars in Germany and got loads of money and were driven around in limousines. Then we'd come back and play somewhere in London and it'd be like the Hope and Anchor which was pretty funny really. But it was kind of important later on for Creation Records because now there was this kind of readymade audience for it in Germany.

EB: There used to be quite a mixture of people down there [the Living Room]. You'd get a smattering of Mods, you got a few sort of Smiths-type bands, a few Rockabillies. There were bands like The Stingrays, The Mighty Caesars, The Milkshakes, all those kind of bands. You wouldn't call them rockabilly you'd call them Hamburg Beatles-type groups, you know, that sort of thing. And yeah, it was a good crowd. I mean it was a good mix. Never violent or anything. It was always sort of up. When we played at Alan's club, the Living Room, we played there a couple of times as The Times.

JF: Yeah, the speed thing came with The TV Personalities. We were all drug fiends. That was a result of being in Germany, really. Well they used to give us all this shit and someone used to go and make all the tablets and shit just to keep us going. One place that we played was like a nightmare version of The Beatles in Hamburg. We played this fucking place in Berlin where they'd opened this new club and we had to play all fucking night. It was completely bonkers, the place was full of trannies and nutcases. There was one guy who was apparently some kind of police officer and he spent the entire night with his head in the fucking bass bin, like, *all night*. You'd get there about half-eight at night and five o'clock in the morning he'd still be there. Being in that kind of atmosphere we sort of gravitated towards a sordid side of life.

EB: One day, Simon Smith who was our drummer had been in The Merton Parkas and he'd been in Mood 6 and turned and said, 'Why do we keep playing this grotty little pub?' I said,

'Because I think this guy McGee is gonna fucking do it. There's something about him.' And Simon reminded me of that the other day. He said, 'You were right about him. You could see the guy was gonna do something.'

JF: The Living Room was just a room above a pub. He would put on gigs at other places. He was doing alright, there was a bit of an underground following for Indie-type bands which nobody really acknowledged at all. As I recall, it was quite an exclusive kind of scene, which then went straight on to being very mainstream. So there was hardly any time for people to get into it as something that was cool. I think that people were frustrated and they wanted something to be happening. People always want some kind of scene to be happening.

EB: Biff Bang Pow, that was the group Alan was in. I thought the first couple of singles were punchy but I thought 'There Must Be a Better Life' was a great record. I think what he did a little later on, about '87 or '88, when he developed a sort of like a Neil Young strain to his writing, I thought that was good. Yeah, I liked his songwriting. I actually thought for a long time that maybe he was the most accomplished writer on the label, although I think Innes brought quite a lot of melody to things.

JF: We got to the gig at the Living Room and I got sent off to get some equipment for all the different bands, so I hired a big estate car and threw it all in the back and when I got there I only had £6 on me, I'm here with ten fucking amps and absolutely completely bankrupt, and I'm like 'I want my six quid for a cab.' It seemed reasonable enough.

If I'd had a pocket full of money I'd have waited till a couple of hours later but you know. I hadn't been warned about him, I'd just heard he was our kind of guy. He was the kind of person who liked the things we liked, you know, liked music and he had

ALAN McGEE AND THE STORY OF CREATION RECORDS

42

a band with a similar kind of thing but nothing really happened with them.

EB: I stopped playing with The Personalities about '82. And then did The Times and my own stuff for about four years until about '86. I'd see him on and off throughout that time. We were just bumping into each other. I'd go down to the office. They had an office in Clerkenwell Road. So around that time, about '84, '85, I was in the office and it would have been Yvonne, Alan's wife. It was basically the two of them in the office running this label. And of course, Dick was there. I always liked Dick. And still do. So we'd come in. It wouldn't be so much hanging out though. It wouldn't be sort of like going out to gigs or anything.

JF: It was all pretty much ready to go, so it was just a question of finding somebody and making a proper record, which I suppose was The Jasmine Minks. I can't remember what order they came out in. I think that was a bit of an attempt to see if it would work, and to do this label he made a completely different distribution deal, and all that. I don't think it was a case of, 'Is it going to work? Am I going to put something out that I've poured my heart into? Is everybody going to say it's shite?' So he just did this thing with The Legend. He just cut a few tracks and put them out. He was quite satisfied with the way the distribution all worked.

JB: He got me out of Devon. He was doing a club called the Living Room and he put out a record which was shit. I was aware of it. I obviously read the music papers and there was something about this Living Room thing that I liked. There was something seedy about it. Although, I didn't know anything about it.

JF: I was pretty much the producer in those early days. We used to use really grim jingle studios and things because they were cheap. We also found that the engineers in the places would very rarely have this thing that they thought of themselves as the record producers.

Because they'd been doing a toothpaste advert the day before, if you went in there with a cool band, usually they'd be delighted. They didn't really care whether they liked it or not, it was like, 'This is great, you've got guitars and bass and drums and shit.' They'd always be really helpful. When we had slightly more money we started using Alaska, Pat Colliers' place, under the arches in Waterloo. I think it's still there, it was quite a good studio and the first proper recordings we did were with The Jasmine Minks. I think they rehearsed there and could get a cheap deal, so we cut them there and then we thought it's only fair to let other people have the same opportunity to cut stuff there. And we got on very well with people there.

JB: I was working in a record shop in Bristol and the back room was a distribution office so everything came in early, all the pre-releases, white labels, and promos. So these white labels from Creation came through and it was The Jasmine Minks, Biff Bang Pow, Revolving Paint Dream. I liked them. They were rough ten-bob recordings, garage records, but I liked them. There was something moddy about it, something '60s about it. It was garage stuff I guess, but accompanying these things were these hand-written promo notes.

Now press releases usually say that 'so and so's from there and they play gigs here and this is their second release, and blah, blah, blah.' The Creation ones were like: 'Fucking play my fucking record, turn off the radio and fucking listen to this NOW.' I liked that. So at that point I got really into it because there was something going on. I was reading more reviews, there were groups like The Stingrays playing there and The TV Personalities seemed to be a getting reviewed all the time. It struck a chord with me at the time. The only other British group around at the time that I liked was The Smiths. I decided at a certain point round then that I was going to go back to Plymouth and I was going to put bands on. I was going to do a club. I was going there most weekends and I found myself a location. I got poached by this HMV shop to go and be assistant manager, so I had this great plan I was going to take that job, rob them blind and set up my own stall on the market selling records. Which I did. Just before I was leaving, I rang this guy up from Bristol, I said 'Hi, can I speak to someone from Creation Records?' This guy whispered 'Who's that?' I said 'It's Jeff Barrett, I'm calling you from Bristol, I'm going to be in Plymouth and I'm starting a club. I want to put some of your groups on.'

A thick Scottish voice replied, 'Are you taking the piss?' I said 'No, I'm not. What are you talking about? Am I taking the piss?' I said, 'No, seriously this is what I do. I'm familiar with your stuff through the press. I know you do the Living Room and I know you do this fanzine called *Communication Blur*.'

JF: I had 10% of the company and I think Dick had 10%, or something like that. I don't know, Alan had most of it, but it was ideal. At the time we didn't really have contracts. It was like a 50:50 split on net which was fairly standard at the time.

JB: *Communication Blur* was a very important fanzine, a fanzine that was as Pop Art as you like. Him and Joe Foster were ranting and raving and shouting and swearing and slagging everyone off while writing about The Fire Engines and about Johnny Marr and The TV Personalities. One of his first releases was a flexi disc with The Pastels and The TV Personalities. It was quite important on the London scene. Kevin Pearce [writer and early Creation supporter] was part of that scene and there was a guy called Simon Bereznik who, funnily enough, I saw the other day walking towards me, dressed as a woman. I was like, 'Fucking hell'. I mean, what do you say to someone you haven't seen for 15 years when they have a dress on?

So I rang this guy and he thought I was taking the piss. He was just a paranoid fucking guy but I liked him. He must have taken me seriously because the next day he sent me through some fanzines and we struck up a relationship. I went back to Plymouth and started the club and I did put his groups on. I put The Jasmines on a couple of times. I liked them. I put The Loft on which was Pete Astor's group with Bill Prince and got on really well with them. Plymouth is a long, long way away but we weren't stupid, we were hip, we knew what was going on. But, you couldn't go and see a band every night so it was a big thing, a big event. We made something happen and suddenly we had a lot of friends. It was a really good crowd and these guys loved it. They used to come down a long way from London to go and do a gig which they got paid nothing for, but they enjoyed it cos it was a responsive crowd and everyone got drunk, stayed at my house and had a good time. So me and McGee started getting on really well and he said 'Come up and stay with me in London'. So I did. I went to Tottenham, just off Seven Sisters Road, me and my girlfriend stayed with him and Yvonne.

JF: Alan was very similar to the way he is now. Enthusiastic and helping people do stuff. If he felt that someone was good at doing something he'd really encourage them. He felt very much like that about all the acts, that they were all great. Every record was crafted and it was a big part of our lives. We had to put them all in sleeves, you mustn't forget that. We used to do it at Alan's house.

JB: To tell the truth I thought he was quite strange. He was very obsessed with music. He had an average record collection. He was obsessed with The Television Personalities, he loved them. But his pad was just like a domestic scenario, two young Scottish people move to London to work. But he wasn't a real drinker or a drug user. He wasn't rock 'n' roll, he wasn't that clichéd or anything like that.

I was a little in awe simply because there was this guy in London putting out records, doing a club which is something that I aspired to. I don't know what I expected. He was a nice bloke and we became friends. He was really good to me. But I expected something wilder I think. Joe Foster was the wilder side of things really. Alan then told me about The Jesus and Mary Chain, we went along and saw them play at a pub called the Three Johns in Islington. They were absolutely brilliant. Mind blowing.

ALAN McGEE

PAOLO HEWITT: HOW DID YOU FIRST MEET THE JESUS AND MARY CHAIN?

ALAN McGEE: Right, Bobby said . . .

PH: Is Bobby still up in Glasgow at this time?

AM: Bobby's still in Glasgow. Bobby hasn't come down yet. He doesn't move down here till the end of '87, till he comes to Brighton. I mean my marriage was – my first marriage – was breaking up because we were like two completely different people. Yvonne wanted me home for my dinner at 7 p.m. and I wanted to be a rock 'n' roll legend. It was the typical relationship. You go out with somebody when you're 18 years old and you've got that bond. By the time you get to 27, you're a nice person but you've got nothing in common with them. So it was one of them.

PH: WHERE DID YOU MEET YVONNE?

AM: At British Rail.

PH: She worked there as well?

AM: Yeah. So I suppose that was one of the things that we had in common with each other. And I think it was quite a competitive relationship in some ways. It was a good relationship and I had some of the happiest years of my life with Yvonne when it was good. But the truth of the matter is that she was a great looking girl right, you know, Italian looking girl, and I think I was a sort of geeky looking invisible looking kid so she sort of had the *power*. In relationships, somebody has the power, you know, whether it be with looks, sexuality, money or power, whatever.

We loved each other but she started dominating me more than I dominated her. And then I started getting famous because of the Mary Chain and really she couldn't deal with that. So the relationship really did fucking start to fall to pieces, do you know what I mean there? So that was kind of the beginning of the end.

PH: SO WHERE DO YOU MEET THE MARY CHAIN?

AM: So what happened is Bob and a guy called Nick Lowe from Scotland . . .

PH: Nick Lowe?

AM: Yeah, not the Nick Lowe. He basically like said to Bobby, you know, there's this band, I've made a tape of them. You might like them but to me they remind me of Generation X, but on the other side of the tape there's this amazing Syd Barrett bootleg. So he gave it to Bobby and he put on the Syd Barrett bootleg and it was fucking amazing. And then he turned it over and he put the tape on and he loved it. And he went 'They're a great band McGee, get them down to your club'. So he told the Mary Chain, 'I've got a pal who's got a club in London and will put you on.' And they were like, I've heard it all before mate. And sure enough I put them on. And they were so great and there was such a great bond between me and the brothers, William and Jim Reid, we just immediately started working with each other.

PH: What bond did you have?

AM: Punk. To be honest they were Punk rockers. I mean, the sound check the first song they ever did was 'Vegetable Man' right. Second song they ever did was 'Somebody to Love' which they never recorded and, to this day, is one of the great Mary Chain unrecorded songs. They should have put that on tape. And they did 'Ambition' by Subway Sect. Along with 'Upside Down' and 'Never Understand' and that was the sound check. And after the end of the sound check I went up, – cos I was kind of like a little bit cocky now and the papers loved me by this point because I had the great club putting out these cool psychedelic records and sub-Punk psychedelic records – and said, 'Do you want to be on my label?' So that's how it started with the Mary Chain.

PH: What did you say to them? 'I can make a record for 200 quid'? I mean what deals were you doing then?

AM: None, it was all handshake deals. That was the joke. Right. Like when around *Be Here Now* [third Oasis album] came out in 1997 and *The Sunday Times* were running these articles about how fucking strict I supposedly was. Do you remember that? I was supposedly the Peter Mandelson of Pop? Paolo, up until 1990, we never even had record contracts with the groups. We'd been going six years. That is not the work of somebody that is a control freak. But we'll get onto that later on. So anyway, it just all sort of like, you know, the label just developed. So what bit do you want me to pick up from?

PH: The Jesus and Mary Chain

AM: The Jesus and Mary Chain, right. So they came down, did the two shows, blew everybody away. Danny Kelly, [*NME* journalist] was in the pub, I don't know if he was upstairs or he was downstairs. I suspect Danny was upstairs.

PH: This is at the Living Room in Conway Street?

AM: It had moved to the Roebuck. It got moved because Conway Street had been shut down. It's at the end of Creation LP 001 *Alive in the Living Room*. Which has got to be one of the worst recorded albums. And Joe Foster recorded it on a 2-track. Fucking . . .

PH: What is it? The last ever gig at the . . .

AM: Yeah. It's just like a compilation of loads of bands that played there. And it's basically taking the piss. It should never have come out.

PH: When did it come out?

AM: I think some time in '84, about a year after the Living Room closed I think. I think. Yeah it sort of closed about then. Or maybe it came out in '85. You'd have to check from the sleeve. I can't remember. And then we brought the Mary Chain down for about four or five shows in September. Alice in Wonderland which was in Gossips. And the Mary Chain were so pissed and they were so nihilistic, they got taken off for their own safety. I was the manager. And I had just met them. And they were so drunk. And it was like they were a danger to themselves and to the public. So they were taken off and at that point I was on a massive, massive Pistols trip. I was living it, right. I was thinking, 'I can't be Johnny Rotten but I can be Malcolm McLaren'. It was immature but at 25, you know, we're all immature. So it was great fun and of course there was the media. London was boring. It was like '84 after all and there was fuck-all happening. Suddenly you had this group of guys that were just lunatics. Like sort of Cramps meets fucking Subway Sect or something like that. And then we put out 'Upside Down' as a white label and the place went fucking mental. John Peel played it for like three weeks in a row basically, you know. Before we put it out there was like 20,000 orders.

PH: HAD THEY PLAYED THAT GIG AT HOLLOWAY ROAD BY THEN? THE ONE THAT ENDED IN A RIOT.

AM: No, that was March '95. And the week that they put the record out I became pals with Jeff Barrett. He was working in this shop with James Williamson, the guy that went on to run Creation Books which I've got nothing to do with. Barrett worked for him in this record shop. We used to send out these fucking press releases that me and Foster wrote and they were like, 'Kill all hippies' and 'Fuck your next-door neighbour'. Just sheer hatred. We didn't realise we were so fucking unique. Because all these other record companies like Phonogram would have press releases that would say, 'The band formed in 1981. The bass player is the brother of the guy in Curiosity Killed the Cat'. Yet we were going 'Fucking shag your next-door neighbour and fuck your granny,' and 'Punk rock lives'. The bile – Foster was worse than me – that we were sending out! Barrett got attracted to it because he liked the music but he also loved the press releases and thought, 'These people are insane'. He loved the Mary Chain. He's a music fanatic, he really is. And he phoned me up and we'd talk on the phone and I liked him because he was such an enthusiast. And I just went 'Come up to this gig'. And he brought himself and his girlfriend at the time, Valerie, up to see the Mary Chain. And the Mary Chain did this gig in a room about the size of this. The Three John's I think it's called. In Angel, next to Angel tube.

PH: IS IT THE ONE AT THE BACK?

AM: That's it. And the bottom line is the Mary Chain were there and there were about 20 people there. But it was all journalists. It was a Thursday night. And the Mary Chain did the set and this was Bobby's first ever gig with the band.

PH: Because he joined as drummer didn't he?

AM: Well they kicked Murray [original drummer] out because he wanted £100 a night and we were like, 'You're tripping mate', you know, it's not the cabaret circuit, it's rock 'n' roll! It's like, you know, you're playing to 20 people. So they kicked him out. And they went 'We'll get a drum machine', and I went, 'What about Bobby?' He was an Altered Images roadie.

PH: He was an Altered Images roadie?

AM: Yeah. I know Clare. If you want to interview Clare I'll give you her number. But so he was an Altered Images roadie. And Titch, the drummer was a temperamental little guy. So whenever he was being a prat Gillespie would fill in. And he would do a Mo Tucker and stand up and play. [Mo Tucker pioneered this style of drumming with The Velvet Underground.] I said to Bobby, come and do drumming. So he came and suddenly it looked like a fucking band cos he was totally cool with his shades and within three songs they had trashed the entire set. The drums were at the back of the room and they were kicking things about and it was all feedback and tangled leads. We then went off to do a tour of Germany with Jasmine Minks, Biff Bang Pow at the top of the bill and The Jesus and Mary Chain at the bottom. Although after two nights we all agreed that Mary Chain should be the top of the bill because they were just the real deal. So they immediately got elevated to top of the bill even though they didn't have a record out. We came back and basically the reviews went like this, 'The most important band since Joy Division.' That was the start of the whole fucking fuss.

PH: HOW WAS IT IN GERMANY?

AM: That was the beginning of the drug phase. It was a turning point when we were flirting with it. We were getting all this cheap speed and we were doing all this Russian vodka. I remember having a punch up with Dave Musker of the band.

PH: WHO'S DAVE MUSKER?
AM: He was the keyboard player in The Jasmine Minks. An intellectual copyright lawyer. Joe Foster can get you in contact with him. I had never really done drugs but speed made me so fucking aggressive and I was so mouthy anyway. And I remember I tried to bottle Joe Foster on tour at a gig one night because he annoyed me so much. I tell you who you've got to talk to for your book and that is Adam Sanderson. I've got his e-mail address. He's now a producer at the BBC. And he was a singer in The Jasmine Minks. And he has got a memory and he will remember a lot, cos he told me things in e-mails recently that I was like, 'How did you remember that?' Cos he told me that he worked at Creation for six months, in the late '80s. I don't even remember him working there.

PH: WHERE DOES YOUR AGGRESSION COME FROM?
AM: Where does my aggression come from? I don't know man. Punk, I suppose, really.
PH: But it must have been there for Punk to act as a catalyst.
AM: I know. I don't know. I mean . . .
PH: Was it the Scottish working class thing? You know, us against the world and fuck the lot of you . . . ?
AM: Aye, it was, it was. When I first came to London . . . Paolo, I was mental. I mean, I'm nothing like this now. I mean, I say incredibly really fucking horrible things to people occasionally but I've got to be really, really, really provoked. But I've got no violence in me whatsoever unless someone's hitting Kate or a close friend. Then I'd defend them but other than that I mean I would never start it with somebody. But I remember when we were first down in '81 and somebody would like say something to me as I was walking in a record shop and I'd just go, 'Shut your fucking mouth or I'll put you through the fucking window'. Stuff like that. And I was like, I think back then and I think, 'Man, that was mental'. Because you don't know who you're saying stuff like that

to. You can really meet somebody who can put you through the window. So I kind of like was pretty lucky to get through the '80s.

PH: Bobby was like that as well?

AM: But I've never seen Bobby get into a fight in my life. See, the only way that he's not been smacked from here to kingdom come is that he's Bobby. And people probably don't belt him. I remember one time at the height of doing fucking Es about '91 when we were in Douglas Hart's place in Kentish Town. We'd met up with Roddy Frame. Roddy Frame now has got the fucking soul of a nice kid but he went from being a sober nice little kid on Postcard [record label] to this pop star who had a huge opinion of himself. And he was a cheeky cunt. Really fucking cheeky. And we met up with him at this club Kinky Disco. Do you remember that?

PH: Yeah.

AM: And after he ended up coming back with me and The Primals. And he said something to me about being old. He said something to Gillespie about his haircut or something like that. He said something to fucking Throb about his guitar playing or, fuck, his hair or something like that, I don't know what the fuck it was. And I remember me, Bob and Throb all going into the kitchen saying, 'He's a cheeky little cunt, we'll just do him.'

It was a serious discussion at four in the morning. Just invite him in here and just do him over.

But I said, 'Look he's out of order, right. But at the end of the day it's Roddy Frame and it's like it's gonna look as if it's about his music or something.' And I reckon that's how Bobby's never been belted. Because he's been so fucking over the top with so many people that you go, 'You've got to have lost your teeth by now mate'. And the bottom line is I do think it's because people basically go 'It's Bobby Gillespie.' I don't think you can get away with being as outrageous if you're not in bands. You know what I mean? Do you not think I'm right there?

PH: Totally. But looking at you now it's hard to detect that aggression.

AM: Being absolutely honest, I think it was coming from Glasgow and thinking English people are soft. Deep down I would never have been like that in Glasgow. In Glasgow I was a lot more in my box. But I think coming to London I had this thing that people from London are a bit soft ultimately and I'm pretty Scottish and a Scottish accent – especially the Glasgow accent – definitely did scare some English people. I don't think it does any more but I think it did in the '70s. Jimmy Boyle and all that came along. You can blag your way out of a lot of situations just by being Scottish, and just talking in a really aggressive way. But there were a few blow-ups that I had kind of like late '80s. And I think that was a lot to do with the fact that I was breaking up with Yvonne. And Creation wasn't going well. And it just ended up in a big punch up.

The famous one was James Brown [ex-editor of *Loaded*]. I ended up fighting James Brown at John Peel's birthday party. I had had three or four fights that year and I'd won every fight so I kind of fancied myself as Muhammad Ali, right. I was cocky, thinking, like, three out of three, you're all soft. I was hurting through my marriage to be honest. I just used to knock people out. But eventually it all came to a head at John Peel's birthday party. I think it was his fiftieth birthday party.

I was going out with this girl called Belinda who was a really, really beautiful looking girl.

She was on the cover of like a lot of Biff Bang Pow sleeves. And Brown said something really snide to me like 'What's the difference between Alan McGee and a rhinoceros? A rhinoceros is better looking.' I replied, 'Very funny, you little cunt.' I had a few more drinks. And, you know, usually if sober I'd not bother. But because I was drinking it just really started getting inside my head. So then I went up to James Brown and I went, 'Ah, so you think you're funny do you?' He replied in a smug way. 'Right.' Little did James Brown know at the time that I'd been shagging his girlfriend. Behind his back. She will remain nameless. So I went up to him and said, 'Well, I just want you to know James, you might think that I'm a cunt but, at the end of the day, every time I fuck your girlfriend she still swallows my cum.' He just fucking, really lost it. This is the girl he was really keen on and I'd been knocking her off. And not only that, but I'd gone up and told him. So the bottom line is James then gets like that. [Alan stands up and mimics the stance that Brown adopted. His fists are clenched and tilted as if ready to pounce.] I had a glass so I went, 'Yeah' and I threw it over him. And it was all over him. I walked away but Brown turned around and walloped me with a fucking punch that sent me against the wall. And then he came at me. He was a little fucking tiger. One of those little guys that is hard to fight. And he was just raining punches on me. So then I started fighting back. But Paolo, I'll be honest with you, I'm glad it got stopped. Because the truth of the matter is, I wasn't winning. It was 60:40 right. And I was glad it got stopped. And at that point I thought, 'You know something McGee, your violence is over and out mate, it's not worth it, you know.'

PH: AND SPEED WAS BRINGING THAT OUT OF YOU AS WELL WAS IT?
AM: It was drugs. It was a lot of E really. You know.
PH: Alan, don't know if you've heard but Es are meant to peace you out!
AM: I know. But . . . Me and James Brown never got on for about two years after that and then to his credit right, we ended up becoming good mates. I think that if you have a *really* bad argument with somebody you end up being good mates. I don't know what that is. Me and Gillespie had that and we'll get on to it later. You don't really know this, but through-out the whole of the '90s, up until about a year or a year and a half ago, me and Gillespie hadn't got on since *Screamadelica*. The relationship dilapidated when he became a rock star. He was really selfish, incredibly self-obsessed. I became a drug addict. And we grew apart.

PH: OKAY. WE'LL TACKLE THAT LATER. LET'S GET BACK TO THE JESUS AND MARY CHAIN. WHAT YEAR WOULD THE GERMAN TOUR HAVE BEEN?
AM: German tour. 1985. No, no, November 1984.

PH: AND WHAT ALBUMS HAD CREATION PUT OUT BY NOW?
AM: Yeah. We did three albums. We'd done *Live in the Living Room*. Then we did *Wild Summer*, which was a sort of pop art sort of compilation. The newspapers slagged it off. Then we did Jasmine Minks which the music papers loved. Then the fourth we did was Biff Bang Pow and they sort of all came out in '84. That kind of made sense financially for the

label because Biff Bang Pow and The Jasmine Minks sold about I think about three or four thousand each.

PH: DID YOU HAVE OFFICES BY NOW?
AM: We had.

PH: WHERE DID YOU ACTUALLY START CREATION RECORDS?
AM: I used to live at 98 Beaconsfield Road, Tottenham N15. And then I started managing the Mary Chain so I got the broom cupboard in Hatton Garden. What was the number? It's right on that corner of Hatton Garden, Turnmills Road, it's on the corner of that road. 83 Clerkenwell Road. I had the broom cupboard and I managed the Mary Chain. And *that* was the Creation office. Me and Foster used to stay up when we were doing a bit of speed. We'd stay up, we'd do a line of speed and put records in covers. But it was so pretty fucking innocent with drugs. It was just so that we'd do the sleeves. It was maybe like three lines to fucking see us through the night you know? So that took us up to '85. And then we signed a load of more bands, you know, like we signed Felt, The Weather Prophets, and The Bodines.
PH: All big groups at *NME*.
AM: Yeah, they were. They were huge fans at *NME*.
PH: They loved them. You were such a hero up there.
AM: All that was great for us. And then *Psychocandy* came out and that was Album of the Year.

PH: WOULD *PSYCHOCANDY* BE ONE OF YOUR CREATION TOP TEN ALBUMS?
AM: Yeah. But it's not on Creation.
PH: Of course, you go to Warner Brothers with the Mary Chain.
AM: Well the reason I had to do it was that Creation was in Beaconsfield Road. In my house. In a private, housing scheme thing.

PH: BUT SIGNING THEM TO WARNER, DIDN'T THAT KIND OF COMPROMISE THE WHOLE INDIE ETHIC?
AM: It did. But they were leaving. They wanted a living out of music and

I couldn't give it to them. They wanted to work with me. So yeah, it was compromising the Indie ethic. But the way I looked at it was, I love this band, I'm probably going to make 40, 50, 60 thousand pounds a year out of being their manager. My house was a £15,000 mortgage in Tottenham. I thought I could probably make another 10 or 15 Creation records from the money that we made out of managing the Mary Chain. So that's why I did it. It made it possible for other stuff to go on. But I wish it had been on Creation because it was a classic album.

PH: I understand that but doesn't your philosophy allow you to have it both ways? There's one part of you that's saying the 'I want to be a rock star and I want the big house and I want all the girls' traditional rock star success stuff. And then there's the other part of you saying 'I wanted to be a Punk rocker.'

AM: But I always saw Punk rock as successful. I didn't see Punk rock as not success. I saw Punk rock as a way to live your life with an edge. I'm an obsessive character, I become obsessed by different things. And I was obsessed with Creation and keeping it going.

PH: SO NEVER ALONG THE LINE DID YOU THINK 'THIS IS IT, I'M GONNA GET THE HUGE FUCKING HOUSE NOW'?

AM: No. Honestly. Never Paolo, I never have, never. I mean, I was putting these records out because I had to do it. It was like having to have sex or having to go to the fucking bathroom. It was like, you have to do it. You know what I mean? It was a need. I thought I can make a little bit of money. I can supplement my lifestyle and I'll probably have a bit more money than my mates because I'm putting records out. I always had money, to be fair. But when I say money, I don't mean money that I could buy a million pound house or something like that, but money that would enable me to go in the pub and buy a round of drinks and buy a girl dinner. It was like that. I never thought that it was going to be anything else.

CHAPTER TWO

ALAN McGEE

JEFF BARRETT: I put the Mary Chain on in Plymouth. They'd only played a couple of gigs outside of Scotland or London prior to that so we put them on down here. I rang up the local radio and the local press and said, 'You know, there's this terrible, horrible group called The Jesus and Mary Chain – blasphemy or what – playing in Plymouth.' Their reputation for being in trouble was already significant enough for me to get local press and radio to road block a little gig. I got the front page, I got on the BBC news and there was a road block. The club was called 'Ziggies'. It was small but it was a really good place just off Union Street which was a horrible street left for the sailors who had been away for months and who now wanted a woman. And it was all provided for. It ain't the same now. It's kind of lost it.

We had these fucking freaky looking people coming out into this sailor world. People were like, 'I can't go down there.' I was like, 'Of course you fucking can' so we did that. The gig was absolutely brilliant. There was this beautiful chaos, that's the best description I can think of. People were not making music like that at that time and it was the sort of music that a lot of people said wasn't music, which is great. They looked great as well, well Bobby did. Bobby looked fucking amazing.

JOE FOSTER: The Mary Chain seemed very much in the direction we'd been going in and this was the combination of it. We thought, 'Fuck it, let's go for it'. Alan was really knocked out by them. He was like, 'This is brilliant, we've got to capture this somehow.' So we just made a deal with them. Fifty-fifty.

We took them off and recorded them at Alaska. It was quite desperate because we were quite short of money so we had to get the session started at midnight. This was in dead time. [When a studio is not booked and allows people in to use it for free.]

Their drums were broken so we had to break into the locker of this band we knew and take their drums and use them – which they were a bit bemused by. 'Why didn't you just ring us up and say can I borrow your drums?' I replied 'It was one o'clock in the morning Frank, I didn't want to disturb you.' He said 'Well, you're a cunt aren't you.' Thinking about it now, Frank would have probably been up at one in the morning. And we did 'Upside Down' and 'Vegetable Man'. It took about eight hours or something like that. But then, yeah, we had quite an outrageous degree of speed. We were all doing it but not so much Alan because he thought it was a bit sordid. 'Upside Down' went mental. I think there were 20,000 advance orders.

LAURENCE: I was in France and I was very obsessive about British music. I would listen to John Peel on Medium Wave – really bad reception and all that – and I heard The Jesus and Mary Chain. I didn't realise that the feedback was not due to bad reception at the time. But I really liked them. I loved it. I was planning on going to London for New Year, so I decided to turn up at the ICA where I knew they were playing. I turned up with my bag and naïvely asked for a ticket and I was laughed at. They said the gig had been sold out for quite a long time. That's a story that Alan really likes. He heard me arguing at the door saying 'You have to let me in, I've come all the way from Paris.' So he gave me a pass and got me inside and said give it back once you're in. Then he came up to me and asked for my number – I don't know why.

JB: Alan asked me to tour manage The Jesus and Mary Chain in Europe. I'd never been out of the country before so I had to get a passport. I was 25. They had signed to Warner. *Psychocandy* had come out and they had this tour in Germany, Benelux and that sort of shit. I didn't know what Benelux was, and I didn't know what a tour manager was. Fucking hell, I had to take some shit. I had to quell riots in Cologne on Friday nights, I had to make sure we got paid for 15-minute sets which, for some reason, the promoters hadn't been informed about. They were expecting two hours and this band comes in, trashes the place in 15 fucking minutes and then leaves with loads of people really pissed off – promoters included. It was horrible. Loads of meat-head German guys.

ED BALL: When Jeff came back from the tour, Alan said 'Where are the tour accounts?' and Jeff brought out loads of toilet paper and napkins, all scrunched up. And those were the tour accounts.

JB: He didn't tell me before I went that I needed to bring them back with me, did he? If I'd been briefed before I went on that tour of what a tour manager's job description was perhaps it would have been different. But I don't think Alan knew what one was anyway. I think he didn't put two and two together; you don't get someone like me to be responsible for your money.

They never told me that a rider wasn't for me for example. So you can imagine: I was on tour with them and they were difficult, awful bastards. It was hard work, it was just hard. Everyone was away from home and I shouldn't have been doing that job, it needed someone professional. It wasn't fun.

I got on with Bobby Gillespie, me and him kind of forged a friendship but other than that I didn't like it, and I was grounded after that. Alan was wiser to it than I was but it was really new to him. Everyone was wingeing it a bit and I think Alan was really enjoying playing this kind of McLaren role.

L: So a few months later I got a phone call at 7.30 a.m. It was McGee saying they were coming to Paris and were going to play Le Bain Douches – that was the hip venue at the time – so I saw Alan again and there were very few people at that gig. But out of this meeting I ended up dating Jim from The Jesus and Mary Chain, so I went to London a lot more. Jim and Alan were such good friends and Alan was so involved in everything, he was managing them but they were very close on top of that. Alan realised I really liked the music that he loved, so that was quite nice. Then I ended up moving to London and moving in with Jim.

SUSAN McGEE: I remember one of The Jesus and Mary Chain gigs, when they turned up at the Barrowlands and it was just unbelievable hysteria from the fans, do you know what I mean? The minute you get in a colder climate I think the fan base is mental.

They were all standing outside and they were all shouting, 'Jim, yeah! William, yeah! Douglas, yeah! Bobby, yeah! Alan, *fuck off.*' So even then he was classed as the manager or, at least, to do with the material side of it.

JB: So in the end what happened was that McGee said 'Barrett, what the fuck are you doing here in this fucking place? Come and work for me and I'll give you a job. If you want to come to London and stay on my floor for a bit till you get yourself sorted. Get an enterprise allowance scheme because I can't pay you any money, but if you get on that you can get your rent.' So I did, I set off straight away. This was the summer of '85. I think I moved August or September.

SM: It was the London Polytechnic gig when the riots happened. At that stage, everyone was spitting on bands. Oh, it was terrible. Jim Reid wore a black mohair jumper onstage and you couldn't see it was black. It had polka dots from the spitting. And did he jump into the crowd? I think he just *fell* into the crowd. And then he started fighting with a guy. And then they all had to pile in and the crowd were all fighting. And then they climbed up on the stage and we all had to run off. We were at the side and we all had to run off and just hide in this dressing room for about two hours, barricaded in. And there was loads and loads of damage. We were hiding behind the barricaded door and Alan said, 'Keep Susan at the back,' and it was like, he's always been like that you know, a really kind of protective brother. And I think there was a big argument because there was a huge amount of damage and who was going to pay for it and whatever. It was good for them.

JF: Basically, we had to get an office so we're thinking 'How're we gonna get an office?' but we didn't even know how to look for an office. I mean where would you go? So, I asked a girl called Juliet Harles who worked for the Alternative Tentacles or one of those companies and she came up with a great idea. Mike Alway [founder of the Blanco Y Negro label] was the guy to ask because he was always smooching around looking at offices and seeing what they were like. So we rang up and he said: 'I've just seen something in Clerkenwell Road and I don't want to be there but it's pretty good. You should go round and have a look.' So we went over and it was a good place to be. Hatton Garden, fucking hell, really impressive. So we rented a cupboard just to get our foot in the door. It was really small and we had an old record player that someone had given Alan. We put it in one corner, a couple of books in the other corner and that was it. One desk, and we'd sit on one side each. Pretty sad really but that was it. It was nice to be able to go and just wander about the West End all day, doing nothing in particular. I would go in record and book shops and just hang out meeting interesting people. Alan loved that.

At that point, I think we were still doing the Living Room and

I think we were doing a club in Soho called the Orgasm, which we used to make a lot of money from. We just had bands on and as long as they were nice people and they could pull a crowd we would book them. So we had all those types of bands, all kinds of trashy bands we had them all on there and made a lot of money out of that. We had The Cannibals, Stingrays, Milkshakes, The Pogues. We made a lot of money out of The Pogues.

JB: Joe and I never got on. He didn't fucking like me. He was not around so really it was Alan, Dick and me. Ed came in not long after. This was at 83 Clerkenwell Road, which was on the corner of Hatton Garden and Clerkenwell. It was the tiniest of tiniest offices. But I didn't know what I was doing and neither did they, but you had this guy who was fucking fuelled up saying 'We're going to be this, we're going to be that.' He was full on. Me and Ed used to sit in there sometimes, unaware of the financial situations that we were close to closing down – everyday. You really felt that it was your *life*. You really wanted to be there and you were glad you were there; you'd do it for Alan and you'd do it for each other. It was really good fun.

JF: The Jasmines played with intensity. Tony Barber of The Buzzcocks thinks they were the best band ever. The Jasmines – not musically but in their view of the world – came from the same kind of odd place that Kevin Rowland comes from; totally intense, where everything's got to be completely black and white. I have always liked that. It was one of the reasons why we admired Kevin Rowland.

JB: From there I started doing the press, I would go and master records, or I'd do a bit of radio. There was no money to employ staff at this stage so we all did everything. This was the time the C86 thing got going and we were right in the middle of it. C86 was this tape that *NME* distributed featuring loads of Indie bands.

The Scream were very misinterpreted at that point. They did a song called 'Velocity Girl' which was the first track on the C86 cassette. It was a big thing. Suddenly there were these really awful, dull groups and Primal got bracketed into that thing. But it was a case of 'Hang on a minute, Primal Scream deserve to be on that *NME* cover mounted cassette as being representative of something that's going down now. But why are they on the same tape as The Wedding Present?'

EB: The early and mid-'80s were a ghastly time for music. A lot of the other labels were bollocks. These labels were run by people who were a good five to ten years older than us and all these people suffered from what I would call – because it's quite common now – that Situationist thing. This whole thing about it's got to be political to be correct. This is PC before PC! They never really took any of us seriously. And also because they probably saw Alan as this sort of like provincial upstart that would go away soon. I think what annoyed them was that every time they thought he was dead and he'd gone to the wall, he'd bounce back again. He was so resilient.

JB: That '86 thing was big, but what was good about it was that we adopted the Scream. I loved Primal Scream – always have done from day one. The first time I saw them play was at a free gig at a student haunt. And they were brilliant! It was The Byrds. It was Love. They were a collection of all my favourite groups. I put them on in Plymouth.

I put them on a couple of times and we used to lose money every weekend. What used to happen was that my mates would put a hat round so we could set enough money to carry on. So when I packed up and moved to London a lot of the guys carried on and the Scream went down. I think they went down twice, actually. It was good they played Plymouth four times. There's a bootleg vinyl album from one of their gigs. I haven't got a copy but it exists. Although you could rattle on for hours to your mates about these groups, about these times, in the big scheme of things, the mid-'80s were terrible times. Aside from black music and hip hop, music was terrible.

Studio technology killed things. Tell me a great British record that was made on a small budget that has got a good drum sound between 1980 and 1990? People in the studios were technoed out of their minds.

So we started our own agency, and I booked the bands out and I managed them. This is how I made myself a bit of money because there was still no money to go round. So McGee said 'Alright Barrett you do that and you can have a commission.' So I'd take 15% of each gig I booked. But I'd end up booking them, tour managing them, and doing the press on them. It was a brilliant crash course. I did press and I set up this agency.

It was all instinctive and for that I thank Alan immensely. He taught me everything and I taught myself everything because he gave me the trust to work things on instinct. He allowed me to do that. I owe that guy tons. To be in a position where you're eager and keen and then to be trusted by somebody – that's something.

ALAN McGEE

ALAN McGEE: I think the relationship between Jim and William Reid started off as a good relationship but by the end of the '80s it really was a terrible one. William got married two or three weeks ago and Jim was the best man but I think that's probably a lot to do with the fact that I don't think William's got any *mates*.

PAOLO HEWITT: WERE THEY AT EACH OTHER'S THROATS WHEN YOU CAME ACROSS THEM?

AM: Aye.

PH: And was that fuelling a lot of the on-stage stuff?

AM: I think that the band took no prisoners. I mean by the end of the '90s I'd been in rehab, Douglas was in rehab and we are waiting for Bobby to go into rehab. And the Reids, I mean, I went out with William a few nights and it was like he was obsessed with women. And I mean obsessed by women.

PH: So you signed them to Warner Brothers because they were going to leave you. Why, because they wanted to be bigger?

AM: Aye.

PH: HOW MUCH DID YOU SIGN THEM TO WARNER FOR?

AM: A lot. They were a great band. They made two amazing albums and after that they sort of repeated themselves. They couldn't change their sound. But it's hard to realise that when you're in the middle of something.

PH: WAS 'UPSIDE DOWN' YOUR FIRST RECORD TO MAKE YOU MONEY?

AM: Yep.

PH: Okay. So what comes after that on Creation?

AM: More Pastels singles. Felt. Primal Scream. And then after 20 releases, we went into proper sleeves.

PH: WHY DIDN'T YOU RELEASE RECORDS IN PROPER SLEEVES BEFORE THEN?

AM: We couldn't afford them. Bobby used to press the sleeves.

PH: Bobby used to press them?

AM: He used to press the sleeves. We'd design them then and we would send Bobby up the design. Bobby, believe it or not, was a printer so he used to get them printed then send them back to us and then we would fold them.

PH: SO WHEN DID THE PRIMALS COME ABOUT?

AM: They'd been kicking about since they played the Living Room in '83, ironically, sounding like Public Image. They were just Jim, Beattie and Bobby. And then the first proper Primal's gig was probably October 1984 when they had the tambourine player. Bobby was the singer in Primal Scream then he was the drummer in the Mary Chain. He was in both bands but the Mary Chain took off first and then at the height of the Mary Chain – after *Psychocandy* – they wanted him to join the band as the drummer. But he wanted to be a singer. So he left the band. You've got to respect him for that. It would have been easy for him to carry on being a pop star.

PH: WHEN DID YOU SIGN THE PRIMALS?

AM: '84.

PH: WHAT'S THE FIRST SINGLE YOU DID WITH THEM?

AM: 'All Fall Down'. Then it was 'Crystal Crescent'. But then the B-side to 'All Fall Down' was 'It Happens'. And the B-side to 'Crystal Crescent' was 'Velocity Girl'. And people always liked the B-sides better than the A-sides.

PH: That's right. In fact, someone was raving about 'Velocity Girl' and the first Primals album in the paper last week. Who was it now?

AM: It was a good album. We played it in the office the other day. Some of the tracks were fucking great.

PH: WERE YOU QUITE INVOLVED IN THE MAKING OF THAT ALBUM?

AM: I was really involved in the first three Primal's albums. And then the one with 'Rocks' and stuff like that I was not so involved. I had nothing to do with *Vanishing Point*. This album, to be honest, I don't think even Barrett can claim this album. It was the band's, do you know what I mean?

PH: Did it do well?

AM: What one?

PH: Primal's first album.

AM: No. It bombed. Number 67 in the chart. It never got released anywhere else. It totally bombed. It was even dropped by Warners. Then it came back on Creation and we gave them a £12,000 recording budget and made another album.

PH: WERE YOU DOING DEALS BY THEN WITH OTHER MAJORS?

AM: We did the House of Love. I started managing The House of Love in '88. And I signed them to Dave Bates' Phonogram.

PH: DID YOU FIND IT HARD MANAGING BANDS AND RUNNING A RECORD COMPANY?

AM: No, no. I've always done it. I think it was quite good for me, managing House of Love. Because, the deal was huge. It was a £400,000 deal. So I made £80,000 out of it and that funded Creation. The other side of it was that I learned how *not* to go about doing things.

Everything that Phonogram had done was almost the wrong way round. I remember showing them 'Loaded' at the beginning of '90 and them thinking it was mad. Then it was a huge hit, you know?

PH: HAD YOU DEVELOPED A MANAGERIAL PHILOSOPHY? I MEAN, DO YOU HAVE ONE NOW OR DID YOU HAVE ONE BACK THEN?

AM: It probably would have been: take as many drugs as the band. Be more rock 'n' roll than the group. I think that was it. It was never thought out but, to be fair, it would have been quite hard to have been *more* rock 'n' roll than Guy Chadwick. I told you before that guy was a fucking monster. Big time. Drugs. Women. The lot. He loved it. He absolutely loved it.

PH: That's funny. I remember him being presented in *NME* as this studenty kind of musician.

AM: I know. It wasn't in the cool way that somebody like Gillespie is. He's never *not* been cool. Five o'clock in the morning and we're in this club and Bobby Gillespie stands in a Ramones T-shirt: a man out of time and fucking dimension. But he's still fucking cool. But Chadwick would shout 'McGee' and you would turn around and he would pull up his shirt over his head and show you his cock. And you're like, 'You're a lunatic, you need help.' I had a lot of good fun doing the House of Love because of it. Chadwick was just basically bonkers.

PH: WHAT DRUGS WERE YOU DOING?

AM: Mostly ecstasy.

PH: With Chadwick?

AM: Yeah, yeah. But he wasn't clever though. I'll tell you something; I took Bobby and Kevin Shields down to Shoom and it changed them. I took Chadwick there and he still wanted to make fucking sub-Velvet Underground records. He wasn't clever. In the promotional tours we just used to go and fuck as many women as we could. So every night we used to try to attract groupies. I remember this time when we were down the Reeperbahn, and there's this one amazing looking woman. I said, 'Chadwick, I'm gonna go and fuck her'. So I go in, have sex with this beautiful 19-year-old German girl and come out. Chadwick's all uptight. So I went, 'Well, who do you fancy?' It's a street full of beautiful women and there's this one woman who looks like a fucking body builder; a bloke in a skirt but it's a woman. Chadwick says, 'Her!' So he goes in and I'm waiting outside in this street and suddenly Chadwick shouts at me, I look up, right, and he's hanging out of the window shouting, 'They don't take credit cards.' I'm really fond of Chadwick. I had some fucking amazing good times with him.

PH: SO LET'S GET BACK TO CREATION. WHO'S WORKING THERE AT THE MOMENT?

AM: Right. What year are we talking about, 1989?

PH: No. We're still in about '87.

AM: Well in '87, Creation nearly goes down the toilet. We do a deal with Warners. Primals, The Weather Prophets and Edwyn Collins all go on to Warners. At the end of '87 my marriage breaks up. I'd fallen out of love with the woman. I was depressed and living in Brighton. Dick's up in London holding the fort and that's when our relationship started to get good. There was no bullshit. And in the meantime I was making The House of Love records. With no money. We had a £100,000 debt, I had £12,000 in the bank and I'd spent that making The House of Love album. It was like all the money on one horse. And it sold 130,000 copies. So we were back in the music business. Great. Then it's me and Dick up until April 1988. And then Ed comes through.

PH: HOW DID ED BALL GET INTO IT?

AM: He's always been a friend to me because he's been in The TV Personalities and The Times. He's like a Mod kind of guy on that kind of Mod psychedelic scene.

PH: Now correct me if I'm wrong, but did he try to put on a version of *Up Against It*, the play Joe Orton wrote for The Beatles?

AM: He did. He was just friends with us. He started by coming in to answer the phone and never left really. We had a sort of rota around that time. We were really hip at this point – My Bloody Valentine, House of Love. We'd get loads of these little foreign girls phoning up the office and we took it in turns as to who would *cop* the girl. Usually we'd get one a week up to the office because they just loved the hipness and we exploited it for all our worth.

PH: So they'd ring up saying, 'Hi, I'm . . . '

AM: And then they'd come by. You'd take them for a drink. Blah, blah, blah. It was quite a good pulling sort of utensil, you know. And then after that we got James Kylo in to do the royalties. Then we moved to Hackney.

PH: So, at this stage, you still haven't got any contracts with groups?

AM: No.

PH: Well, if you can remember, what would a typical day in the Creation office be like?

AM: Well, I was only half-time in London. Half the other time, I was either in Brighton or Manchester, or I'd be coming up on drugs or coming down off drugs. I'd be having visions or be signing bands! We never really adopted a business attitude probably until '92.

PH: So your philosophy was take drugs and go off and make an album.

AM: Yeah. We were just mates with the bands and we put records out. But we always owed people money. We always paid but we had a terrible reputation for not paying on time. We had a good reputation for being honest, which we were. We never really knew from one day to the next how we were going to get through it, you know, financially, so we were living total hand to mouth. So the idea that we'd end up selling millions of records one day was never really on the cards.

PH: MY BLOODY VALENTINE, HOW DOES THAT COME ABOUT. AND ALSO, WOULD *LOVELESS* BE ONE OF YOUR TOP TEN CREATION RECORDS?

AM: Ah definitely. They were sort of the 'dog's arse' of Indie. In 1986, they were really rubbish. Joe Foster found them for his own little label Kaleidoscope Sound. He thought they had something. He signed them, brought me to see them and I thought they were sort of shitty. In '87 I went to see them again and they were still a bit dodgy.

Then '88 we did a gig with them. Dick and I said they had to support us. We thought they were so dodgy that they could only support Biff Bang Pow. So we saw them play at Husker Du prior to our gig. Fucking hell, it was like, fucking hell man! How raw is Kevin Shields? So we said, 'We'll do your records'. And that's how we signed them.

PH: WERE YOU IN BIFF BANG POW THEN?

AM: Yeah, yeah.

PH: Right. So who else was in Biff Bang Pow?

AM: Me, Dick, Dave Evans and Ken Hawkins. Instead of trying to be pop stars, we just liked a bit of fun, you know what I mean?

PH: SO YOU SIGNED MY BLOODY VALENTINE IN '88. WHAT WAS KEVIN SHIELDS LIKE?

AM: Not mad. He changed.

PH: Did he? How did he change?

AM: I think it was the drugs, man, to be honest.

ALAN McGEE AND THE STORY OF CREATION RECORDS

75

CHAPTER THREE

ALAN McGEE

JEFF BARRETT: I think Alan had a bigger manifesto than I knew at the time. It was all part of his Malcolm McLaren thing. That was very exciting and it really was just enthusiasm as opposed to manifesto. And then, completely by chance and coincidence, there was this string of killer singles which went bang at the time. There was 'Terese' by The Bodines, there was 'Velocity Girl', 'Up the Hill and Down The Slope', which was the last Loft record and 'Cold Heart' by The Jasmines. It was never set up like that but we had this string of records which really did give us a big break. Although those records sounded quite different it was cool that they were on the same label; it made people think, 'Fucking hell, this is interesting and that label's bang on.'

LAURENCE: Manipulating the media was something quite instinctive. The Malcolm McLaren thing was there, but I don't think Alan's first priority was to imitate him. He realised that his way of doing things was quite close and it was probably later on that he thought, 'Yeah, Malcolm McLaren'. I think it is something that really suited him . . . his whole personality, regardless of McLaren. I think that if McLaren had not existed he would have gone ahead and done what he did anyway.

JOE FOSTER: We were the new Motown. Fucking great. This is fantastic. Wow. We're a really big deal. It was all a scam which, oddly enough, did work in other territories because people in

Germany or France would read the music papers and they really would think we were the happening thing.

JB: As press officer I think I probably talked too much. I just went in there and used the word 'brilliant' too much. I think that it worked because I wasn't lying. I'd just go into the music papers and say 'Honestly you've got to fucking see this band, the gig last night was amazing.' And I wasn't lying. Thankfully, people thought I was a daft bastard and that I wasn't trying to give them shit. I think that's what people saw in Creation.

JF: It was basically the drugs thing driving me fucking psychotic. This was 1986 or '87. I worked in and out. I'd pop back and work with somebody until it started to get on top of me and then I'd be off again. There'd be specific projects I would work on, like Kaleidoscope Sounds, which I was doing with Tony Barber. Tony was just trying to keep me on the wall of humanity. I had completely lost the plot. I could come up with something really great that other people could work on but I couldn't do it myself because I didn't have the attention span. But I would also go off like that [clicks fingers] and start punching people. It was quite funny to watch because I would take on somebody who was clearly three times my size and I would win. It was like how the fuck did I do this? I suppose it's quite funny to think about but it wasn't that funny to go through. I just went completely mental. It's difficult to put my finger on exactly what it was. I just went fucking nuts.

I think Alan was pretty concerned I was going to die but I think he felt a bit better when I started doing stuff with Tony. Tony and I were doing things on a very small scale.

JB: Alan became very . . . well he's always been competitive, but he suddenly became *very* competitive. I couldn't work out if it was to make a lot of money. I don't think it was. He knew about Factory Records and he knew about Mute Records and about

Rough Trade Records being the big independent labels of the day and he wanted to be up there with them. He wanted to sell more records than them. I almost think it was a Punk thing as opposed to a greed thing.

ED BALL: By 1986, I had spent so much money on my records that I had to go and get a job. I was working at Peter Jones's department store which is in the opening scene of the book, *Absolute Beginners*, and I thought, if I have to work anywhere, let it be there. One night I went to see some band at the 100 Club and Alan was there and he asked what I was up to. I didn't tell him that I had a shit job, no money, no life, no girlfriend, etc. I said, 'Things are fine.' He said, 'Well, why don't you come down to Brighton? Come and do some recording for Creation.' I thought, I can't believe he's asking me to do this. Of course, I went down to Brighton.

JB: Felt, The Weather Prophets, Scream and Meat Whiplash were on the label. Things changed a little. There had been a lot of personal stuff that I wasn't really privy to because The Jasmines had been around for a lot longer. I think because The Jasmines had been around for some time they thought they deserved better attention than the other groups. But they weren't really making the records. They had great dreams. They thought they were going to be huge. But they weren't. They were a shambolic mess half the time. They wrote some really good songs and were crucial to that great run of singles in '86 with a brilliant song called 'Cold Heart'. And they made a good album. But they weren't going to be The Scream.

Then Alan thought that Pete Astor was the next Bob Dylan, and he ended up doing a deal with Warners. He took out a double page advert in *NME* for The Prophets album. I think it said something like, 'The Best Record You'll Ever Hear' or 'The Best Record Ever Made', something like that.

A little bit over the top. Alan fuelled Pete's ego to the point of ridiculousness. I remember McGee saying to me one day, 'Oh, Pete said can you stop talking to him so much.' I never understood that one. Actually, I did a little bit. It was Alan tiring of me a little. I've got a big gob and I had my own ego coming through as well.

EB: So he was getting the new roster together and it was people like House of Love, Felt and the Primals – all the way through there are the Primals – Jazz Butcher, Momus, all these new bands and he said to me, 'Look, let's make a record and let's make something a bit darker than the kind of stuff you've been doing. Why don't we come in and do it with you?' So Alan played guitar. I did all the basses. Alan had a fairly good line in raunchy guitar at that time. He'd discovered the Les Paul and he could do that kind of howling thing fairly well. Dick was sort of more like the bloke out of Echo and the Bunnymen.

I would just do my John Lennon, chugging slightly out of time. It worked nice. Mulreany [drummer] just held it all down and we made an album called *Beat Torture* by The Times. And that was good fun. It took a week to record and, during that time, he kept saying, 'Look, we're gonna expand the label.' At that point it was back to Dick and Alan because, you know, he'd split up with the wife. I started answering phones, dealing with Rough Trade and a whole host of other stuff.

JF: I always found the Rough Trade people really childish. I'd always be meeting these idiots and there'd always be something or other, some big fucking mood and it would take ages to figure out what it was. It was usually a row with somebody's drummer about seven years ago and that's why they were acting like this. I found it all really weird. Even if I'm meeting someone who punched me in the mouth seven years ago, I might be a bit wary in case he does it again, but I'm not going to be telling everybody, 'This guy's a fucking maniac!'

EB: You'd walk in the office and there was just two desks we used to fight over. But I've never met anyone like Jeff Barrett in my life because he was hilarious. Absolutely hilarious. He used to say to me, 'So are you going down Shepherds Bush to do the soft shoe shuffle, tonight then, you old Mod you.' He's just a brilliant guy. So it would be Dick, Alan, me and Jeff. A typical day would consist of: 10 a.m. come in, ring up Rough Trade, get sales figures daily, 'How many did we sell of this? How many did we sell of that?' Then Alan would ring at about half ten and say, 'Tell me the sales figures. What have we done?' So I'd go through it with him. Alan would probably come in about midday and tell us if he'd seen a band or sometimes we'd have a bit of a chat and then we'd get Alan saying, 'Right I want this done, I want to do this.' Alan was very thorough about everything.

If things didn't work out, if things weren't happening like he expected then he could explode, and I was really surprised to see this very gentle sort of Scottish fella explode into a sort of Glaswegian devil. He would sometimes just go fucking bananas. It surprised me but it didn't shock me because it was his label. It was his vision. It was his original idea. And he had the most to lose if it all went.

JB: I don't know whether he changed. I think I was quite in awe and incredibly happy that I'd got a job, but as his profile and his label's profile went up – when he did the deal with Warner in 1987 – suddenly Rob Dickens' name was mentioned more times than Malcolm McLaren's. I think Alan thought, 'Wow, I'm here,' as opposed to, 'Right, I'm here and I'm really going to screw them right up.' He took the money from Warner Brothers and I think it hurt him when he got dropped. I don't think he could handle the failure of being dropped by Warner.

EB: I would say that he's driven by the thought of people not taking him seriously, not believing that he could make things happen. I think all the way through our lives we all come across people that don't believe. Maybe his was the toughest gig of all because it was the one where he constantly faced bankruptcy. I think he was driven by that. I think he was driven by searching for love as well.

See, we weren't even thinking about the charts pre-'86. House of Love was starting to gear up the charts but we never really spoke about the charts. It was never to do with that. I suppose it's money. It's the security of having money. All the things that maybe working class boys want to get so that they never have to worry about the bills. It's a composite of things that drove the man on.

JB: A lot of the records at the time did have qualities to them; a kindred spirit forged in the face of adversity on a low budget.

EB: It was manic. Why was it manic? It was manic because there was about ten, twelve bands, some of which he was managing as well. And that meant dealing with them in a tour capacity. We had the budget for like one band. It got really manic when the House of Love released 'Shine On' and 'Christine' because they became a big act at that point. I liked them. In my head they were like Lou Reed. I saw Lou Reed here. You know how you have to apply a criteria to what you like? For me, if I can find it somewhere in that integral area between '63 and '68. Then I'll buy into it.

JB: Ed was very secretive. Ed didn't give out his phone number or his address. We didn't know anything about Ed in all of this. He's very eccentric. I liked him a lot, he made me laugh. I hope he liked me because we had a very good time. It was good. It was *funny*. Anyway, in 1987 I started my own label, Head, signed a group called Loop and left Creation for a bit. Then I came back, started another label, Sub Acqua.

EB: Alan was never short of targets. If he was gonna try and get The House of Love into the Top 30 when they were starting to peak as a high profile independent band then he would do it – and he did it. Did I like all those things though? I kind of felt that a lot of the bands, a lot of the records, I'd seen it all done with The TV Personalities.

I'm not knocking these bands but that kind of shambling, what we'd call now the Indie-ness of them, didn't enthral me because I'd been in studios loads of times and I wanted to make proper records. I wanted to make real records. Like someone once said, 'Gigs are for now but records are for ever'.

JB: We were all pretty much on the same wavelength, all pretty much into the same thing. What is a very important piece of the whole picture, which is still the way I hope I live my life now, is that everybody there, the bands, the people who worked behind the scenes were all *totally* into music. People were always coming in with new records. Invariably those new records were actually old records but the conversation always revolved around the cut of your trousers, this Stooges album or whatever. Everything revolved around the fact that we were fans. It wasn't until a bit later when other things started coming through that you started thinking, um, don't know about that. But I liked it all really. There were a couple of things we put out which I didn't like but you were fighting for something that was so naturally what you were all about, so you could go up to Danny Kelly at *NME* and go 'Blah, blah, blah,' with absolutely zero experience in how you do that job, but enthusiasm, genuine understanding, belief and love for what you were doing.

EB: It was a reasonable wage. I never went without wages. A couple of times I put money back, you know, money that I'd earned out of records I put it back into the label. But that's only because I figured I would never have got the money if he hadn't given me the chance to make the records in the first place.

JB: My label stuff is actually quite peripheral but I guess it's important for the McGee mindset. I had a label called Head and I think that in retrospect I didn't discuss things enough with Alan. I'd kind of found my own thing. I think he thought that I was getting too big for my fucking boots, which I probably was. At Creation it wasn't like 'This is what your job is and this is your wage cheque.' It allowed me to think for myself and to operate that way. The natural progression was that I started, initially, doing my own things as well. It started to cause a bit of friction. Mentally, we weren't as close as we used to be and we didn't talk things through properly. I think I wound him up. Anyway, what happened was that Dave Harper who had an office upstairs came down and said 'I'm leaving the Factory label account. I'm going to work for RCA. Do you want to do their British press?' Now I really liked New Order and I quite liked Factory and I was chuffed as it was a major thing for me. Like fuck, this is what I do now. So at that point I struck this deal with Alan: I could operate doing his press, doing Factory's press in the office there.

So that's what happened. I kind of became my own person inside the Creation set up. And that was the start of the end I reckon.

ALAN McGEE

ALAN McGEE: I went mental. And really a lot went out of the window from about '88 to '94. Yvonne left me when I was a demon-fucking drug addict and a reprobate. That was the time that I really ran riot because I was doing a lot of drugs. I was living on my own, I was 28 and I had a little bit of money. I'd bought a flat in Brighton initially. Then I started going out with Belinda. But I never moved in with her until the end of '89. Two years living with Graham and Bobby Gillespie. We went mental. Absolutely mental. Believe it or not, Primal Scream – I know it must be hard to believe now – were a girls' group. They were a huge girls' group. Honestly, one of the biggest pulling groups ever. Gillespie. Big time. And Innes, even. They did these tours and these women would show up from all over the world.

Then what happened in April '88 was that Innes gave me acid for the first time in my life. It was never the same again. Then ecstasy came up in June '88 and it was just fucking bonkers.

There was this Malaysian girl, I can't remember what her name was now but I used to go and do ecstasy with her. And I did it with her for the first six times. I thought I was in love with her. And then I went and did ecstasy with Ed Ball and started having the same feelings for Ed Ball so I suddenly knew, 'Fuck, this is *the* drug.' But believe it or not, it took me about six months to get into Acid House. Even though I was doing ecstacy from June. The only reason that we would go to these clubs right was to get the drugs. The minute we'd got the drugs we'd go back to my house and we would drop the drugs. We never went for the music. We thought the music was shit. And then I went up to see New Order at G-Mex. And I was kicking about with this girl Debbie Turner, who's like a total face up there a real mad girl.

PH: I know her, blonde girl from Manchester

AM: A real character: a lovely, lovely girl. Basically, within about the first five minutes of me being up there I said, 'Oh, can I come back and stay at yours.' And she went, 'I don't know about that. Let's see'. Up to that point I always had this quite hostile relationship with her because I'd always been like the Primal's manager so I was always kind of the dad of the band. Her pals were going like, 'He's a fucking lunatic, watch yourself.'

So I ended up at 7 a.m. doing the most humungous amount of drugs. I was chatting up this model, I think she was called Hayley. Duffy [Primal Scream band member] ended up going out with her. And I thought I was doing quite well with her. Then suddenly her head became this green diamond. And the reason it became this green diamond is because I was on about two or three E. I had been talking to Pat Nevin [footballer] in the downstairs area of the Hacienda which was called Disorder. Ironic, since we had just seen New Order. I saw Shaun Ryder. I'm mates with Shaun so I went up to Shaun and I said 'Look Shaun, can you sort us out with some drugs. More drugs!' He said, 'I'll give you half of this.' And I'm thinking, 'I'm on about fucking three as it is, what the fuck do you mean "a half"?' It's the only time I've ever had a Fantasy in my entire life. Have you ever had it? That's some drug, man. So he puts half of this tablet in my mouth. I'm home with Hayley and suddenly I said 'Your head's just become a green diamond.' So she fucks off. I don't know if you've ever nearly overheated on an E? I got a scary one. I started thinking I was overheating. Dick went and got me loads of water and I stopped drinking alcohol. Drank water and the rushes stopped.

At a later stage they were walking me through the basement underneath the Hacienda and its pure Acid House. Suddenly, those beams were fucking little psychedelic, symmetrical shapes. Green little diamonds and blue circles. Everything was really symmetrical. And perfect. It took me about four hours to come down. Tony Wilson was sitting decked out in white satin as if he was the king. And Peter Hook was sitting down there. Shaun Ryder was coming through trying to pick up all the women. And at 7 a.m. I realised that Debbie Turner was still through there. I immediately thought, 'Fuck, try and cop.' So I've wandered through and I have a look at Deborah Turner. And she's dancing to this Acid House music. The light suddenly goes on. That was it. Party was over and suddenly I understood Ecstasy and Acid House. I get it now. I tuned into that. December 21, 1988. That was it. Acid House. Then I went on up to see Happy Mondays play January 1989. Me and James Williamson went up. And we went in to the Hacienda. We'd been in some Indie club to try and get women right? The bottom line is, sure enough, loads of Indie girls were all coming up and they're all dressed in black and it's really boring. And it's the same records you've been hearing for the last ten years. Dinosaur Junior. And it's fucking boring right. But I just discovered the party. I knew what it was about. And I went, 'Let's go to the Hacienda. Let's get some E.' So we walk in. The whole club is absolutely jumping. Everybody's having a good time. Everybody's burning the fucking pathway to the Hacienda. Completely friendly. This guy would stop the record. 2000 people put their hands up. And in the middle of the floor. There's a guy. It's Shaun Ryder. Punching the air. Sweating. I just thought, 'This is it. I've arrived, man.' So, I immediately moved to Manchester.

I had a proper weekend, you know, round the different drug dealers' houses. In London it was sporadic getting E because all the E was probably coming down from Manchester anyway. So I got a flat above Factory. And it was just fucking great, you know what I mean? Tim Booth worked underneath me, right? And this was the fucking joke. He used to complain about 'disco music' that I was playing and that guy ended up having a fucking Indie dance hit about two years later. I mean musically it was a really interesting time because we started making dance records. I mean a lot of dance records. We found Fluke, we found Dreadzone and Danny Rampling.

PH: YOU PUT OUT DANNY RAMPLING TUNES?
AM: Yeah. We put out 'I Hate Hate'. Do you not remember that? We

were the first to put out Danny Rampling records. Love Corporation put out tons of records. Ed did this Love Corporation thing. Weatherall did a remix which the Chemical Brothers, to this day, still say is one of their five favourite ever tunes. Instead of it being a case of Tim Buckley, singer songwriter, suddenly it was Turntable Orchestra: Frankie Knuckles, Todd Terry and Juan Atkins. So Creation reflected that. But I was still doing Indie records. I was still signing Ride and I was still signing up bands like Swervedriver. House of Love and everything like that. So I was still doing these kind of bands. But musically it made me go like that.

We moved out of Hatton Garden right about April 1989 and moved into Hackney in the same summer. We had a sort of opening launch party. Danny Kelly was at it. And I think that was the party that turned *NME* to fucking drugs really. To E really. Because I don't think Danny Kelly or Helen Mead had ever been on them before. We definitely turned Helen Mead on to it because she'd never been on an E. And basically, we had this amazing room at the top of Hackney right. It was full of mirrors and it had a fucking glass roof and all the debauchery that ever happened in that building happened in that little place. We had one house tape that we just put on and on and on again. And it was just fucking debauchery. The entire label was lying about, Sheilds, Gillespie, Mark Gardner, Danny Kelly, and fucking Jack Baron, the Manchester posse. All mates, converged. It was just a fucking mad one.

PH: WHAT SORT OF THINGS WENT ON?
AM: To be honest sex wasn't really part of the agenda until 9 a.m. when it was like, 'Okay, well who's left standing?' I was with my girlfriend, Belinda, I was starting to get closer with her. I'd been seeing her for about six months. She was a party girl.

PH: WERE THERE ANY BANDS YOU MISSED BECAUSE OF THIS EXTRACURRICULAR ACTIVITY?
AM: No. I got most of them. The only one I'd say I missed in that period was The Stone Roses.

PH: HOW LONG WERE YOU IN MANCHESTER FOR?

AM: Six months. No, nine months. I had the flat for about nine months. And then Paul Mulreany drove me down. By the end of September 1989 I drove all the stuff back into Brighton. And then by about November 1989 I'd moved in with Belinda up in Birmingham. But I was still off my tits. I mean when I was with her in Birmingham I was calm but when I was in London, I was just running riot.

CHAPTER FOUR

ED BALL: Primal Scream are the jewel in the Creation crown. They were there at the start and perhaps they weren't making ground breaking records but they were at the end and they're making fucking amazing music still, they are one of those incredible bands that have always put adventure above career in what they wanted to achieve. But they still keep going, still keep getting up and still keep coming back again.

JEFF BARRETT: Meanwhile, the Primals made this second album which nobody liked. Absolutely nobody. At that point, one of the best pieces I could get for them in the Melody Maker was Innes talking about guitars in the section at the back. But I was doing a really good job on My Bloody Valentine, whom I really liked. They put out this single 'You Made Me Realise' which was fucking brilliant and it was round the time of the House of Love singles and I did a really good job. It's nice because I saw Kevin Shields the other week and he said, 'You made the record'. Then Alan sacked me. 'I need to meet you,' he said and, forever the classic guy, he arranged to meet me in the Pizza Hut at the top of Tottenham Court Road opposite Centre Point. He told me that I was sacked. I saw it coming.

So I said to him, 'Can I continue working with the Scream and the Valentines?' He said, 'No.' So I said, 'Well can you at least tell them that I wanted to?' He never did. In fact, he actually told the Scream that I didn't want to work with them and that's when the shit kicked in.

LAURENCE: And one day out of the blue I got a call from McGee asking me, 'Have you got a job at the moment?' I went 'No' and he goes 'Do you want to come and run the press department at my office?' I went, 'But I don't know nothing about the press!' I met him and Ed Ball. It was the least predictable interview I ever had in my life because it was very much me sitting down there and coming up with arguments why they shouldn't give me the job. I was saying I didn't know anything and Alan was saying, 'Rubbish, you love the music, you have attitude and you are going to do it.' So I said okay and I started working at Creation about three weeks later. I was the only girl.

They were based in Hackney at the Westgate Street office. Alan, Ed, Dick, James Kylo, the accountant, Brendan and me. That was it. Sometimes Paul Mulreany would come in and there was this endless trail of very nice girls.

EB: Girls used to ring up, especially girls from abroad. It's true. It was unbelievable. They used to ring us up and say, 'Is that Creation Records? What time are you open?' Because I wanted to come by and buy a couple of records'. I got thinking, 'This is a record company, I mean, it's not a record shop. Yes. Come by. Yes.' So that's what would happen.

JB: I was sacked in the fucking Pizza Hut on the corner of fucking Charing Cross Road. I mean come on man have a bit more class than that please. That was so unceremonious especially since I'd been there for four years or something like that. That is a fucking long time. We *had* drifted, admittedly, but to be sacked in a Pizza Hut, do you know what I mean? And to not have told the Scream that I wanted to continue working with them. Bobby Gillespie went off for a bit. I said to him, 'Why are you so weird? You do know that I told McGee that I wanted to continue working for you?' He was like, 'No, he told us that you didn't want to work with us.' McGee you're a fucking weirdo.

I think he has got a vindictive streak in him but I am not sure if I want that to go in your book. You see, I don't think I was disrespectful. But maybe I was and maybe what he was saying was, 'Go on, you've got your own baby now, go with that.' His social skills are quite odd really. He was moving faster than me and was operating on a totally different level. Maybe I was a little disrespectful, maybe I was talking more about the

BOBBY – ROCK 'N' ROLL STAR

BOB G – THE DEXEDRINE KING '99

OPPOSITE PAGE

TOP: BOBBY – JAPAN '91

BOTTOM: PRIMALS POST-COMEDOWN '97

MARY CHAIN – LIVERPOOL ST. STATION '98

**SUPER FURRY ANIMALS –
AS WELSH AS MARK HUGHES!**

FANNIES CIRCA '91

**NORMAN BLAKE SPORTING
A DODGY MOUSTACHE '96**

ALAN – THE COCAINE YEARS

Mondays, New Order or East Village, than I was about his stuff.

I think the key thing was Acid House. He had a revelation. McGee came back from Manchester and said, 'Barrett you've got to try this ecstasy – it's fucking great!' Alan wasn't a druggie, that was the mad thing about it, but this thing changed everyone's lives, none more so than his.

EB: When I was working at Peter Jones I had a bit of a mini-revolution myself. I used to hang out with these guys in the post room and they used to be playing all these Chicago House records and there was one record in particular by Nitro Deluxe, 'Let's Get Brutal'. It was an amazing record. I went down to meet Alan and I said to him, 'I'd love to make one of these kind of records.' He said, 'Well, put it on.' And he listened and said, 'This is revolutionary. It is the future of music but I don't know how we could do it.' Then Alan started going up to the Hacienda and he told me, 'I'm really getting into dance music. I fucking hated dance music until I started doing these E.' I said, 'What's that?' and he goes, 'Oh, it's this fucking amazing drug,' I remember we all went up to the Hacienda and there was Tony Wilson, sprawled all over these parachutes, holding court. This was a man that I'd always seen in a suit and tie.

L: Basically Alan had employed a trail of people. Mick Houghton was doing it for a while, then he went to Jeff. I don't think Alan was wrong. When I started working with Creation they were going through a period when the whole Manchester thing was starting to soar. Jeff was much more interested in his connections and with what was hip and happening. There is always a period when you lose your inspiration and motivation, and Alan didn't like to be second best after all the other projects that Jeff had. He didn't really help. I didn't know anyone in PR and I was left to my own devices. Jeff was the last person I would have been able to phone. I think he realised very quickly that he shouldn't have let it go because one of the first records I worked was 'Loaded'.

JB: What happened at that point is very, very crucial because we couldn't get the Primal Scream record away to save our lives. But it wasn't my fault. I was doing my job, it really wasn't my fault. Nobody liked it, that was the grim fucking truth of the matter. I got pilled up and I got out and I made friends and one of them, Richard Norris, said, 'There's one guy you gotta meet. You've got to meet Andrew Weatherall because you'll fucking click like that.'

So I thought okay and we met and we clicked. Richard was right and we became good mates. Andrew was doing Boys Own Magazine, and I gave him the Scream album and he rang me the next day saying, 'Fucking hell, there are two fantastic ballads on that, 'I'm Losing More Than I'll Ever Have' and 'Just Too Dark To Care'. The rest of it I'm not bothered about but those tracks!' Anyway, Helen Mead was live editor at NME at the time and I had this idea: Weatherall likes the stuff and Helen Mead is totally into this Acid House stuff so why don't we get Weatherall to review Primal Scream? We went to Exeter and Andrew did a live review. Now the Scream had been reluctant to do ecstasy; they thought it was stupidness. I got them pilled up – eventually – down in Brighton. They had a party down there and I took this tape with Joe Smooth, Marshall Jefferson, Blaze and Easy Street. The Primals were, 'Get it off. Get the fucking Dolls on. Get the fucking Stooges on.' There was like a war, you know, 'Stick that back on you fucking boring old cunts!' and it was great. 'Put The Dolls back on.' So after this they met Andrew and they did eventually get it. That's how I got them together.

DJs were starting to remix at the time. Paul Oakenfold was starting to remix rock tracks. Weatherall and Innes clicked like that. Innes is a genius a total genius, he is completely fucking brilliant. And him and Weatherall went into this studio, up in Walthamstow and turned 'Losing More Than I Ever Have' into 'Loaded'. And the rest is fucking history.

MARTIN KELLY: What no one ever mentions is that McGee

turned the idea down. I was there when Jeff rang him and asked for some money to put Weatherall in the studio. McGee said, 'Barrett, you're bonkers; they're a rock band.' It went to and fro and even Bobby got involved at one point. In the end McGee gave him £500 and Weatherall turned in 'Loaded'.

SM: The whole thing was just all taking off. Alan gave me four white labels of 'Loaded' and he says 'Pass them around to all the DJs in Glasgow.' I played it and thought it was unbelievable and just gave them to all my pals. So it would be my fault if they hadn't made it with 'Loaded'. What a track.

JB: I wish we'd had a better relationship between us because we did something there.

L: Instead of spending over a year getting to know people and getting people to accept me, 'Loaded' dropped me in at the deep end. I had people calling me all day. I walked in and I was very lucky. That whole Acid House thing was something that Alan really enjoyed. The music was secondary because he was more interested in the culture. People wanted to go out, get loaded, and have a good time. Just like the record said. Alan has always loved to see people interact around Acid House parties. I probably missed the most interesting ones because I had a boyfriend waiting for me at home. But Alan made sure everyone had a good time, giving away ecstasy like there was no tomorrow. God knows how he managed to communicate. I missed a lot of the wilder stuff because it was lads orientated. There was a lot of after-hours activity at the office that I couldn't really join in. I had to go home and he would get really pissed off if I wasn't going home.

There were quite a few girlfriends working at the office. Karen was seeing Bobby and Christine was going out with Andrew – the Primal Scream girls.

CHRISTINE: They were probably the best times of our lives.

KAREN: They were so special.

L: There was this hilarious time when we started ordering courier bikes on Fridays which would go and get the supply of E for the weekend. We would do a little intercom call on the office saying 'Who wants some of this?' People would call me on my line and say, 'Yeah, I'll have two' or whatever. We ended up ordering a bike and putting reference TRIPLE X in the courier log book. Then the E would be delivered to the office by a poor courier. It was like a big party and we were working, but the motivation was due to the fact that we were very much part of a big adventure. There was a brilliant vibe. It was funny. No one could believe the things that happened. We were still in utter financial shit. I even threatened to resign to get my expenses paid. On a regular basis I was throwing fits at the office. It was really hard.

EB: I enjoyed the . . . I don't like the syllables in debauched, so I enjoyed the *candidness* of the parties. It didn't feel as if anyone was gonna die. No-one was gonna get hurt. Underneath there was an old sweat shop. You would go upstairs and there would be the first office, then there would be another office around the corner then there would be a little room up the top that had a sofa bed. Alan rented the next house. He had two houses and just knocked a wall through. Downstairs from there was a bed which is where Teenage Fanclub would later have their bed-in for *Bandwagonesque*. The party would go on all over the place.

If you were tripping you would be walking into different rooms. You'd have a My Bloody Valentine room where they'd all be sitting in the dark. It would be smokey and the fug of the smoke would give you a hit. Then you'd walk into another room and that would be like the drinking room or something. And then out the back would be the heavy ecstasy room. Suffice to say, you'd find that the Primals would be represented in *all* the rooms. And then you'd have Guy Chadwick wandering around indulging in total exhibitionism. If it all got too extreme in the heavy ecstasy room then you'd come back into the Valentine's room and you could just chill out. But the best room was the one that you'd have to access up a very ornate little spiral '60s staircase leading into an office that had a balcony. Everyone would head for that room at about 4 or 5 a.m. as the sun was coming up. The walls were just completely mirrored all the way around. So we either used to do our best Acid House dancing in the mirrors or would just sit on the balcony and chat. Alan reminded me of a very, very warm version of Andy Warhol. That's probably because he often used to wear this stripy T-shirt and he would just be talking about music, 'I just want to make good records. That's all I want to do.'

There was never any trouble but if there was I found it was usually some of the girlfriends of a band would be the ones who would be stirring it up. Drugs didn't help. It would bring everyone together at the start of the evening but about four hours later and it starts to get a bit snide and there's people starting to take the piss. And then two hours after that, you know, someone's girlfriend has like trampled over somebody in another band and then it's going off – not real fisticuffs because most people in bands are sort of nonces – but screaming and shouting.

SIMON STEPHENS: We went away on tour and then when we came back, Creation HQ had gone from Indie haven to a party freak shack. It was just going berserk.

EB: When Alan introduced Guy Chadwick to that culture he released a demon because he was just unstoppable. It was as if it had all been building up waiting to go. He just went bananas. It

ALAN McGEE AND THE STORY OF CREATION RECORDS

would be almost a regular occurrence at Creation parties that at some point Guy would just pull his trousers down to his ankles and just stand there like that. Makes you think of Syd Barrett or someone like that, doesn't it?

L: A girl called Fiona was Alan's assistant, a girl called Kle ended up becoming Alan's PA. After that Karen turned up. It was coming to the end of innocent girls hanging around just because they were cute. They started to show some initiative and get good jobs.

K: The first time I ever met Alan? Well, there's my version and there's Alan's version. His version is I went up to him at the Milk Bar, and said, 'Give us a job,' and he said, 'Start Monday'. Then he walks into the office, sees me sitting behind the desk and says, 'Who is that girl?'

Well, what really happened was that about a week before that I had met Fiona Clark at a Lilac Time gig. Fiona was working at Creation and she said, 'Oh yeah we need a receptionist, why don't you come in next Monday and start?' I was fresh off the boat from Canada and said, 'Is there going to be an interview?' She said, 'No, just start but if you want to meet Alan, come down to this bar on Wednesday.' So this was the story before my first Monday morning in his office.

I arrive at Creation in Hackney, this totally unglamorous area of town, just above a Turkish sweat shop. This place is so weird, I thought. Every office and every department is on a different floor and the whole thing was a maze. I just thought, this is mental, and I'm answering the phones saying, 'Morning. Creation,' to people from Sire Records in New York whilst thinking, 'Wow, do they know what place they're calling cos this is so weird, so haphazard.'

L: I'm French, and I have a mentality and a way to interact with people which is very different from English people – I am much blunter and I haven't got the ways of the English people. Alan is very much like that. Alan and I could relate and it was a closeness we kept all the time. He wasn't the boss; it was Alan. When Alan came back into the office, suddenly everybody would feel really motivated.

I was thinking about it a couple of days ago. If there was a time that I was feeling really depressed Alan would give me the energy and I'd eventually just go 'Fuck it, I'm going to go for it.' I like that. It's very much an attitude I like. He has got a unorthodox way to do things. I think he has a very good instinct. My lack of knowledge of how to do things as a PR was and is probably my biggest asset.

K: In terms of their finance, I wasn't privy to that kind of information, but it seemed OK. Ride had just done pretty well with 'Nowhere' and My Bloody Valentine were making the record that everyone was all excited about. Soon after that there was the Primals and we signed Teenage Fan Club which was a great thing for me because I've always loved them.

L: Ride were these very nice clean-cut kids from Oxford. Their lives had been very non-eventful and they didn't have that many ideas or opinions in any way. They were quite normal, quite bland.

Ride were not the best at interviews and we were always trying to find an interesting way to get them to come across because they were quite boring. On the other hand there was this intellectual side to My Bloody Valentine that very few bands managed to get. Kevin Shields was seen as a real brain, an intellectual person. There was that real aura about them. Musically, people really appreciated Ride, but I had a big problem with them. That's when I realised that PR involves a lot of things.

K: I was one of the very few people that was hired into Creation who wasn't a friend of Alan's. You know there was Christine who'd gone out with Andrew from the Primals; Laurence who'd gone out with Jim from the Mary Chain. I felt very outside of it; like little Miss Goody Two Shoes on the outside who didn't have a clue and could never go to all-night parties and take loads of drugs.

I didn't have the constitution to handle it and I was a little too intimidated at the time. Everything still functioned as a company but everyone would go out, get absolutely slaughtered and come in late the next day. Alan would be off his face a lot of the times and you'd never know what kind of mood he'd be in the next day. I remember one time he phoned up someone in the office and their line was engaged so I just paged them over the intercom and said to Fiona, 'I've got Alan for you on line two.' After that every single person in the office phoned me in reception saying, 'How did you do that?' They were all genuinely amazed that someone had figured out how to use the intercom. We didn't have a franking machine so I'd have to go and borrow a trolley and go to the Post Office with three boxes full of records. They'd all be teaching me how to speak Cockney and I'd sit there and lick stamps and it would take an hour out of my day. Then I'd come back and someone would have something urgent to post. I'd start doing things like sending – a big thing – saying, 'I'll put a little box in reception for post. Anything that's in there by 4 p.m. will get posted that day. So if it's important make sure it's in that box before four.' Then all of a sudden things started to obviously work a little more efficiently.

I pretty much put it into shape. I did reception for about three months before Alan pegged that, 'Hey, I think actually she'd be a good person to organise my stuff.' At first Alan didn't really like me. He just used to say, 'Who's this Canadian girl in reception? She's crap.' And everyone would be like, 'No, please God no, you're the first good receptionist we've ever had, please do not let her go.' The irony of it now is that he's one of my best friends. But it didn't start off that way.

L: It was one of those things where I'd been there for a long time and I wasn't motivated. I didn't understand what Alan was doing anymore. I was always well treated, but the link with Alan wasn't there anymore. The lads attitude thing got in front of the whole show. This coincided with Tim Abbot being brought into the equation. Tim is a lad. And he brought with him a sexist attitude. There was a lot of showing off, which it had not been about before. Music, and finding it amazing, was over. I really started backing off. I didn't really see the point. Every band we were signing, every record that was released, we were all behind it so much. Then Alan signed Superstar and I thought sometimes you might not get the band that will blow people's minds.

SM: He came from Levi's. And women! My God, I don't know what woman would fall for Tim Abbot. I thought he was a nice guy. But thank God I was Alan's sister, do you know what I mean? He knew not to come near, so I didn't even feel threatened. But I was lucky.

EB: This is where we come to another important part of Alan's character. There's something in Alan's head that makes him sympathetic with people who are unhappy in what they're doing, unhappy in their lives. He would see somebody and say 'Do you know what? You'd be brilliant doing this, why don't you do the marketing at my record company?'

Tim will explain better for himself but as I recall Tim had been working for something like Walkers or one of the whisky people and I think it was all a bit too strait-laced for him. So Alan said, 'Look, come and do the marketing for me.' I think Tim was very good for the company. He had a kind of sassiness about him that made his ideas right for the time. I think maybe Dick was at a point where he was settling with his family. I think he might have just had a second child. And for a good couple of years, Tim was the right-hand man.

K: I just saw through Tim from day one. He was just an opportunist; somebody who used to give Alan drugs and all of a sudden gets himself this job in marketing. Everyone else was being doled out all the work and he was going out and taking all the coke. I did feel really protective towards Alan about that because Alan always did see the good in people first. Tim and Alan would have fun in the beginning; he was a good person for Alan to have around because he had somebody to go to LA with and take loads of drugs and stay up all night. But was it healthy for him? Hell no. When Alan became sick, Tim mistakenly thought this was his chance to come in and seize more control. I was really relieved when he became transparent to Alan.

SS: He was a total fucking fly-boy. He came in with his flow charts. Before that if someone brought in a flow chart you'd piss on it. Tim came in with his flow charts and his vision, and he had a bit of a background. I thought he was hilarious just for that.

EB: I think Tim was good with the marketing and came up with a lot of good ideas. They put out an awful lot of records as well, which was always a problem. It was far too much to be able to concentrate on doing every one of them properly. And a lot of records came out purely because they'd do about four or five thousand and keep the company going.

SIMON STEPHENS

SIMON STEPHENS: I was working for an agency in Tin Pan Alley in Wardour Street and working for a guy called Richard Cowley. Alex Nightingale [Primal Scream manager] got me the job. I'm originally from a council estate in Brighton. I grew up with Alex Nightingale in Brighton. The Primals moved down there. They all had their leather chaps on. We used to see them in the local pub with all this leather gear on and we were like Casuals, early Acid House Casuals and we used to punt a few fucking pills and stuff. My dad used to sell pills to Keith Moon down in Brighton at the Regent, so when I got involved in all this pill selling, he didn't say, 'Don't fucking do it.' He said, 'Be careful, the Cockney boys will come in and undercut you and you'll be out.' And that's exactly what happened. The beginning was when the Scream used to hang out in this boozer with all their leather gear and we used to go up there at night, and I used to be a cheeky little sod and slap Bobby's arse. Through that we used to take the piss out of them but when I saw the band I thought, 'Fucking hell, that is fucking top-notch. This is one of the best bands that I've seen for ages and ages.' One day, this was when 'Loaded' was a white label someone rang up and said, 'Primal Scream have lost their tour manager, he's had a breakdown, we need someone to do it.' I've gone from the other side of the desk and said, 'I'll do it.' He's like, 'Go on. Alright, you've got to meet Dick Green and Alan McGee at the Mary Chain gig at the Kilburn National.' I've gone home to a bedsit to Willesden, told my girlfriend that I was off to Greece, McGee gave me £150 in cash and tapped me on the back and said, 'Good luck son.' I said, 'Where's the band then?' He replied

'They've said they'll meet you down at Gatwick at four in the morning.' I got the milk train down and started to think, 'What have I done here?' I've got a passport, £150 and I don't really know these cunts. I don't know them at all. So I meet up with them. Throb's got his suppository of liquid coke up his arse, Toby, the drummer at the time, is a real big geezer going [crunches his knuckles] and Bob comes up to me and says, 'You don't know what you're letting yourself in for, but I'll make sure it's alright.'

PAOLO HEWITT: DID YOU GO TO CLUBS WITH BOBBY IN BRIGHTON?
SS: You didn't go to clubs, you only went to Schoom if you were in the know, and luckily Andrew Innes went and he let the rest of the fucking world know about it subtly. And then the Brighton side came through and McGee would come down and score some E and we'd all get back to James Williamson's and be there until the morning. There'd be my pals there, then there'd be the Casuals; a cross-section of people and they were all on the same buzz having a fucking great time. We used to do warehouse parties down there back in the summer of '88 when it first kicked off. We used to pack a warehouse, charge £2 on the door. to Bobby used to come. I came with my bird this one time. She was a Swedish model; she had amazing form, you know what I mean? Bobby looked at her. Later on, he told me, 'Stephens the only reason you got that job wasn't because you're fucking good at it, it was because of your bird's legs. We wanted her legs in our dressing room every night and the only way we could get her, was to get you.' I hope that wasn't true.

PH: WERE YOU INVOLVED IN THE HACKNEY OFFICE PARTIES?
SS: I used to work from the office, I used to go off on tour then come back and you'd go into the office and wouldn't leave for three days – you'd even kip in the office. I don't know if you've spoken to Duffy or any of that, but you'd have me and Duffy fucking various people all over the building.

PH: WHAT DID YOU MAKE OF ALAN?

SS: I was petrified of McGee at first. I had this job and I cannot believe my luck, I'm going off to America, I'm going to Japan and I'm going everywhere. I suppose I started thinking, 'When am I going to slip up there,' cos I knew Alan McGee was a professional man and he didn't get where he was without having good people around him. McGee always used to shout, but that was probably something to do with what was going on and the comedowns. I didn't really take on board what was going on, I just went in, tried to do my job. And I think I showed him a bit more respect than he really wanted. He wanted someone to come in and go, 'Let's do it! Fucking go for it!'

ALAN McGEE

PAOLO HEWITT: YOU SAID BEFORE THAT YOU WOULD BLACKMAIL YOUR ARTISTS. . . . COULD YOU TELL ME MORE ABOUT THE PSYCHOLOGY OF MANAGEMENT?

ALAN McGEE: No, well, I knew all my artists inside out. I could emotionally blackmail Kevin Shields to give me records. But my tactics with other bands was just to take as many drugs as the bands and make them love me for it. And even though the bands weren't rich they were having the best fucking time. I mean there was always millions of women kicking about. There were loads of drugs. There would, invariably, be a swimming pool full of girls; half of them from the office, half of them topless, swimming about and doing lines of coke in the pool. Me and Abbot were always at the controls. At the end of the day you had the choice of being at Warner Brothers where everything was really uptight and corporate, or you had this mad fucking bloke who had a swimming pool and got you shagged and gave you loads of drugs.

PH: WHAT ABOUT ABBOT? WAS THAT A CLOSE RELATIONSHIP?

AM: Really, really close. Abbot, to his credit, was solid. Tim made me realise that I had to sort out the money side of it and get some money for myself. This was in 1991. We were round at Abbot's flat with about five grams of coke and Abbot basically said to me, 'How much money have you got?' And I went, '£2,000,' and he said, 'Fuck off, you've got to have at least half-a-million and you've got all these hits!' I said, 'No, I put it all back into the company.' And he came up and he gave me a hug. And he went, 'You're a geezer because you believe.' I thought it was strange.

I thought, 'Maybe the guy's right. I've made all these people rich and famous.' I mean Bobby was off signing £75,000 fucking publishing deals and I was putting everything that was coming in from Creation back into Creation. I mean, if I had a nervous breakdown in '91 Paolo, I was out of the game mate. Because I only had £2,000 in the bank. I had no money. I was living without a parachute. And then that's when I started really thinking about doing a deal. And maybe that would be one of the greatest things Tim ever done for me.

PH: WHEN DID YOU MEET TIM? WHEN DID HE JOIN THE COMPANY?
AM: The first time, from what I can remember, I ended up back at his house. Me and Bobby Gillespie ended up going up to see St. Etienne doing a Heavenly night in this little club in Birmingham. And Barrett was there as were the Manic Street Preachers. I pulled the barmaid and her mate. We ended up with Terry Chemical and these two women and going back to this house which was Tim Abbot's house and we got sorted out by all these women – one way or the other. And that was how we met Tim. And he looked as if he was in Duran Duran. He had long hair. Whenever I was in Birmingham, I used to hang out with Tim. We started going to a few clubs. Me and Belinda quite liked him. We thought he was a funny little guy. He was a character. And then he put this proposal to me. He was always coming to me with his business proposals like fucking tacky marketing strategies. But we agreed that Creation wasn't running right and he should come down and try to get Creation on advertisements. Paolo, he never got me one. But at the end of the day he sat next to me and we just ended up becoming pals. He wasn't a popular man at Creation. He'd kind of get his flowcharts out, you know, like these marketing people get their flowcharts. Except instead of saying, 'If you do this, you get this', he would pick on the fattest person in the room, draw them and say, 'You eat too much.' He was fucking bonkers. So, of course, everybody hated him. I loved him. Dick really did not like him because Dick saw him ultimately as a fucking threat.

Dick was busy being a family man. I was absolutely out of control over Belinda. We were in a decline in the relationship by this point and so, basically, my only chum was Abbot. We kicked about and did shit loads of drugs and had some amazing times. We were always off in L.A. doing business, but what we were really doing was shagging American women most of the time and doing loads of drugs. We'd go around the Viper Room and I'd get on one and then I'd ask every available woman back to the hotel. I don't mean the best-looking women. We'd pick out every available woman in the place. They'd end up back at the Mondrian and just sit up and do all the gear. We'd be sitting with a mound of fucking gear and so it would be about like 16 people there. And me and Abbot. And I'd be on the table in one part of the room. Abbot would be on another, dancing to Led Zeppelin or dancing to The Waterboys or dancing to The Clash. And the mound of cocaine would go down and down and down until at 7 a.m. when there was fuck all left. Then I'd look around and say, 'Where are all the fucking women?' Abbot would go, 'Fuck knows'. That was the story of me and Abbot. That was when me and Abbot realised, 'This is going wrong, man'. It was getting to the point where we were losing the plot. Mark Gardner [Ride singer] was always coming to L.A. with us because at this point he was the biggest sex symbol in fucking Indie rock. He was our mate. So we'd go off for a week to Los Angeles, which didn't help the schedule very much. And then, we'd be sitting in L.A. and be saying, 'Right, do you want to go to Brazil?' And Tim would say, 'Alan, we'll be killed. We will actually get killed if we go to Brazil,' because if we behaved there like we did in America or in England we'd just get fucking taken out. At that point we were really abusive. Abbot was worse than me: I would just tell people to fuck themselves; Abbot would punch them out.

PH: YOU WOULDN'T GET INTO FIGHTS?

AM: Oh no. Abbot was handy. I've seen Abbot beat guys while eight people are pulling him off. He's a nutter. Abbot is a fucking nutter. When I sobered up all these years later, I thought, fuck me, we were on the fringes of being absolute gonners. I think that if we'd ended up in Brazil, there was a good chance that we weren't going to come back.

PH: WAS HE GOOD FOR THE COMPANY THOUGH?

AM: That's a really hard question to answer. I think he was. I tell you why I think he was probably right for the job. He was good for me because he made me think about doing a deal.

PH: WERE YOU STILL COMPLETELY INDEPENDENT AT THIS TIME?

AM: Completely. So it was good for me because he made me think about going and sorting a deal out for myself. Until Abbot I never had anybody marketing in my life. Marketing was evil. But the bottom line is, he managed to get bands to say 'yes' by giving them a line of cocaine and then showing them the most awful piece of artwork ever. I mean Primal Scream agreed to having a fucking Confederate flag on the front of their record cover. And you cannot say that Abbot was blameless in any of that.

Was he good? I don't regret my time with Tim Abbot but it had to come to an end. I think Tim will be a bachelor until the day he dies. He will always have five women on the go. He will always be a fucking party animal. And I don't want him to stop because he loves doing that and I love that he's still doing that. But he was ultimately a terrible influence to have around me. I've sobered up. The bottom line is that I had a bad drug problem and you can't really have your partner in crime – and he was my partner in crime – experiencing the same problems as you. It ended in a not particularly good way between me and him. But I don't have any bad vibes towards him. I suspect when you talk to him, that he'll have a few warts-and-all stories about me. The saddest thing was that I met him with Malcolm at the Groucho Club about two months ago. He's always got a different woman and I've never seen him with the same woman twice in the last six years. And of course it's a new one and she's from America. She's blonde and it's the usual scenario. I introduce myself 'I'm Alan, I used to work with Tim,' and she said, 'So you're the one!'

PH: WHY DID YOU FALL OUT?

AM: I thought it was lack of faith. I was always the one who said, 'Look

I will pull us through, trust me'. And I think that he got scared and wanted a safety net of some kind, like shares, do you know what I mean? At the end of the day, the deal was always going to be a risk.

We went through a very rocky time just before the split. Tim had a direct line to me and I was having my nervous breakdown at the time and he was *squeezing* me at that point. I thought it was wrong. I mean, it is forgiven, I don't hold a grudge and I genuinely have no bad feelings towards him. I suspect he might have some towards me. But he shouldn't have because he's gone on and had some fucking amazing success on his own. He does Fat Boy Slim. He marketed Oasis when the marketing of Oasis was good. When Tim left the fucking marketing for Oasis went downhill. Abbot's marketing was always cheeky. 'Young, dumb and full of cum', 'Sorted, snorted and sported' – these are all my sayings. But I would probably never have put them on an advert if Abbot hadn't persuaded me. So he played a big role in it all. And then he managed Robbie Williams. Tim's had his own success and good luck to him.

PH: SO WHEN DID YOU SIGN THIS DEAL?
AM: With Sony?
PH: Yeah.
AM: September '92. We were going bankrupt.
PH: But you had a hit with *Screamadelica*.
AM: Yeah, but no international set up.

PH: WERE ALL YOUR RECORDS JUST BEING SOLD IN BRITAIN THEN?
AM: Yeah, and maybe 20,000 Primals in Germany.

PH: SO HOW DOES THAT WORK? DID YOU GO TO OTHER RECORD COMPANIES TO DISTRIBUTE?
AM: We were with Virgin in France who were good but distribution was proving difficult. We were going bankrupt and either I was going out of business or I was going into fucking clock one of them. I mean at this point I didn't even take a wage out of the label. I never took a wage

out of the label until 1992. For the first eight years I did not take a wage and neither did Dick. Do you know what I mean? We were living off of being managers, you know?

PH: Who was Dick managing?

AM: Me. I was managing St. Etienne and Primal Scream up to March '92. But it never took a commission but I was the manager for the first eight years.

PH: I read an interview with Bobby and he said that he signed a 50:50 deal with you.

AM: He did, yeah. Up until '92 we did the 50:50 deal. And then after Sony came in we did the points deal. Although the Primals still retained their 50:50 deal to this day.

PH: DID YOU HAVE A 50:50 DEAL WITH ANY OTHER ACT?

AM: Everybody up till '92.

PH: With every act that you signed?

AM: Yeah.

PH: That's pretty cool.

AM: It is cool but it doesn't work. I'll tell you why. The 50:50 deal is angled towards the artist. The artist gets a bigger share of the royalties which means when you have a big album the artist inevitably wants to take four years off. Most labels, if you're lucky, only have one or two bands that pay for everything else, like with Creation, Oasis paid for everything and Primal Scream paid for itself. Everything else lost money. That's the nature of the beast. It's like Mute and Depeche Mode. Every time Depeche Mode don't have a record out, Daniel has to lay 20 people off. And Factory, it was all about New Order. New Order took five years off. The label folded. So a 50:50 deal looks the right way to go about doing business but in reality it's really difficult for a label in the long term. Although I tell you one thing. I bet you Noel Gallagher wishes he had a 50:50 deal with Creation. Because it wouldn't have been 20 million coming into the bank it would have been 40 million.

ED BALL

ED BALL: The problem is this – three great albums, *Screamedelica*, *Bandwagonesque* and *Loveless*, but why are they all coming out at the same time? I think Creation bands are like the women who work in an office; they all have their PMT at the same time, they all put out their best album at the same time. Arguably these albums are the best albums by those three acts. I think it says something about the way that in the two years leading up to those releases, they'd been very close to Alan. When a band is close to the central man of the organisation they usually do their best work.

PAOLO HEWITT: WAS THE MAKING OF MY BLOODY VALENTINE'S SECOND ALBUM, *LOVELESS*, TRAUMATIC?

EB: Yes. Alan would be over in the States trying to flog a band to someone and he'd get on the phone and say, 'Play me the tape down the phone'. It would be a track like 'To Here Knows When' which is the most difficult thing to do, I mean if you listen to it, it has none of the normal rock orientation of instruments. And we were playing it down the phone! And he's saying, 'Are the speakers right, Ed? You've got good ears. Tell me, what's going on?' I had to tell him, 'Well it's, it's a very, very ambient piece of music and the vocals are lost in the mix. Deliberately so.' And Alan goes, 'Oh, my God. I've spent a quarter of a million pounds and I can't hear the vocals.'

PH: It must have caused a lot of friction between Alan and the band.

EB: I believe with that the album title says it all. *Loveless*. It was basically a battle between Alan and Kevin. Not a battle as we understand it but it didn't make sense how they could spend so much time in studios and show nothing. It didn't really figure. And Alan would be saying, 'Well, where is the record, where is the record?' And Kevin would be saying, 'Coming soon'. And the first single to come off it was called 'Soon'. And then it was, 'When do I get the album?' And the next single was, 'To Hear Knows When.' And then when he'd actually got all the tracks done he called the project *Loveless*. Really, it was like Alan playing midwife to this work of genius from Kevin Shields. And Kevin is still at it. When he signed his production deal for an enormous amount of money, do you know what the first song he gave them was? A version of 'We've Got All The Time In The World.' I doubt if he's given them anything since.

ALAN McGEE

ALAN McGEE: I think Kevin Shields smoked it too much. I mean Kevin was getting stranger and stranger and stranger, by the minute, to the point I couldn't work with him any more. But after he left me I think he had some sort of nervous breakdown. He built a 16-foot fence round his house so that nobody could get in. He saw one of his neighbours sleepwalking one early morning in his garden. So he built a huge fence. *Colditz.* Round the house. He then sent his sister out to get green barbed wire to put round the house. He said, 'You can't go on holiday until you go and get sandbags.' So he sand-bagged himself in. And at that point the band left him. And he was pretty happy because he was saying to himself, 'Nobody can get in.' And I said to him, 'Kevin, who would want to come in?' And he went, 'You're right.' That's when he realised it was fucking desperate. He'd built this thing round himself and nobody wanted to fucking come in. And after that it all got very weird. I think to this day he still thinks he's been abducted by aliens. He never went to sleep for about a year. All this mad shit.

He obviously can function on a level. He can come, play guitar but I don't think he'll make another My Bloody Valentine record ever again. But in the meantime he's taken £500,000, I think, off Island, approximately a quarter of a million off EMI Publishing and approximately a quarter of a million off Warner Brothers in America. And none of them have ever heard one piece of music. And the best bit is – he thinks – *it's their fault.* Which I love. I love him. He's my friend. But I wouldn't want to be in business with him again. Only because you become the enemy.

PAOLO HEWITT: WE SHOULD TALK ABOUT THE MAKING OF *LOVELESS*.

AM: Absolutely. Because I was never allowed in the studio for the first two years.

PH: HOW LONG DID *LOVELESS* TAKE TO MAKE?

AM: Two and a half years.

PH: THEY WERE IN THE STUDIO FOR HOW LONG?

AM: Two and a half years making it. And after two years I phoned him up and I went, 'Kevin, you've got to let me in the studio man. I've nearly paid £200,000 for music that I've never heard.' And he used to keep me in the room outside the studio, and not let me in. And I tried every which way to manoeuvre myself round him. Eventually I phoned him up and I said, 'You've got to let me in the studio man, you've just got to let me in.' I emotionally blackmailed him. I went, 'You're gonna make me bankrupt – you're taking the whole label down – you're so selfish.' And eventually he didn't want to but he let me in. Then we started slowly closing it. It takes Paul Weller and Noel Gallagher one day to master a record. He took 13 days to master the record. You cannot take 13 days to master a record. It is an impossibility, you know. So after that I just said, 'I can't work with you any more, Kevin. You're a lovely man.' I still love him but I can't work with him. But you know something – genius – he is a genius. I mean the other artist I would say is the genius of the fucking plot is Liam. Because he's the rock 'n' roll star. Best British rock 'n' roll star ever. But Kevin is the genius architect musician.

PH: HOW DID YOU FEEL WHEN YOU FINALLY HEARD *LOVELESS*?

AM: Angry. Embittered. Treated like shit – I can't explain to you how hard it was working with the guy. I had Dick re-mortgage his house for them. I spent every penny I had in my bank account. We spent £270,000 on an Indie album for a band that had no real fanbase. We almost bankrupted ourselves. And I remember Dave Stewart walking in the studio and Kevin having a few words with him. Dave Stewart walked out and then Kevin turned to me and shouted at me. And at that point I just went, 'You're out.' In my head, I just thought, 'I'm not going to tell you that you're out tonight. I'm gonna put the record out and then you're out of my life. You're a nightmare. I know it was hard for you making this record but that's because you're bonkers. Dick's re-mortgaged his house; you've nearly given me a nervous breakdown; you've had me in tears about three fucking times during this record and at the end of it you cannot even say thanks. You talk to Dave Stewart and tell me to fuck off.' The minute the record came out I just stopped talking to him because I just thought, 'The record's out now, I'm arsed'. He really didn't want to leave the label. And then I phoned him up about five days after New Year. I just phoned him up and I went, 'I can't work with you any more.' And then the next day eleven record companies tried to sign him. And Island won. And it cost them £500,000.

PH: And they haven't had anything since?

AM: Nah.

PH: And you heard that album and you thought?

AM: Not worth the effort. I was in too much pain. The guy drove me mental. He drove me literally to the fucking edge. I mean he's an obsessive genius but in five years I got two records. Nobody's ever got two records out of Kevin Shields. But you pay the price. You become the enemy. He was a fucking absolute fucking fruitcake. And in recent times I think he's got a lot better. I think he's sort of back to where he was on Creation. I think in the mid-'90s he was absolutely out of his mind. When he was talking about getting abducted by aliens that's the point I went, 'I love you mate but you're fucking bonkers.'

PH: And their first album cost?

AM: Two months. £7,000.

PH: WHAT HAPPENED? I MEAN YOU PUT HIM IN THE STUDIO ONCE BEFORE. WHAT'S THAT ALBUM LIKE?

AM: It's great. Really, really good. Great songs. Lacking production. But Loveless fucking production, nobody's made records like that ever. In America, he's a legend. I'm not taking the piss. Both albums did about 100,000 over there. People in America absolutely idolise that guy.

Completely. If I had to summarise Guy Chadwick in one sentence I'd say, 'The guy was completely deluded for who he was'. He had a nanny, a cleaner, a house that he couldn't afford. If I had to summarise Kevin Shields in one sentence, I'd say 'Irish as you could possibly ever be, in the great tradition of the true fucking Irish genius,' which is a quotation from the bible according to Shane McGowan. Shields is a true genius. And his vision is so futuristic and so ahead of what anybody else ever went for. I tell you why he changed. People, after 'Isn't Anything' said you're a don, a fucking don. And up to 'Isn't Anything' he was always considered a fucking second-rater. And he went from being a second-rater to being the first division right, and then it just built up. And then by the time *Loveless* came out, he was the greatest. He's the greatest artist as in 'artist' I've ever worked with. No doubt about it.

ALAN McGEE

PAOLO HEWITT: LAST TIME WE SPOKE YOU MENTIONED TEENAGE FANCLUB. SO WHEN DID THEY COME INTO THE PICTURE?

ALAN McGEE: They were friends with us because Norman used to be in this band The Boy Hairdressers when we were kids. Then they fell out with Fire Records and they wanted to come to Creation. So Bobby again brokered the deal because he knew them. So we ended up like doing this deal with the Teenage Fanclub and we put them in this studio in Liverpool. Now at the time I thought I had two big albums. *Screamadelica* and *Loveless*. So one day I go on up to Liverpool to that studio, I can't remember where the fuck it was recorded but it's the one where the Bunnymen used to record all their records. I went in and they played me a mixed down version of *Bandwagonesque*. Every fucking song was a fucking hit. And suddenly I was saying to myself 'McGee, you don't even have two important albums here, you've got three important albums.'

PH: WERE TEENAGE FANCLUB PARTY BOYS AS WELL?

AM: The drummer was bonkers by the end of it. Do you remember him? Brendan was bonkers man. He was fucking totally gone. But no, I think they quickly distanced themselves a wee bit with the drugs. They'd walk in and whereas the Valentines and the Primals would be on the table with me, punching the air with a bottle of Jack Daniels saying, 'Let's hear it for the Clash. Let's hear it for fucking Scotland,' the Fanclub were a bit like, 'This guy's bonkers and he's gonna try and sell our music'.

PH: WHERE DID YOU FIND THEM?

AM: I didn't actually find them. Dave Barker found them. And he signed them up and put a record out on Paperhouse. And I then started working with them and made *Bandwagonesque*. And that album was one of the biggest shocks to my system ever. This was '91. I had the *Screamadelica* thing happening. Now that album was really a compilation of singles and some extra tracks that we'd fucking fudged together. No matter what bullshit is spoken about that album they were off their tits and we were trying to pull things together. We had no idea we were creating history. No fucking idea. We were just capitalising on the moment. We needed to get an album out. Five of the tracks, 'Loaded', the Andy Weatherall remix, the Sire track of 'Slip Inside This House', 'Come Together' and 'Higher Than The Sun' – which appears twice on the album – had been out before. It's a compilation album right? And it got presented as an album.

So I got *Bandwagonesque*. I had Europe and Geffen had the rest of the world right. I did about 200,000 my side of the world and they did about 200,000 their side of the world. So they'd done about 400,000. So there was a huge expectation on them. More than any other band on Creation. The press fucking loved them. They went silver in Britain. They'd done respectable business everywhere else in Europe. It was ready to fucking pop. It was really all ready to fucking pop. And then the band spent a year in the studio in Manchester right with some guy that did The Who remixes right, and I'm talking about The Who in '91 right not The Who in fucking '67. The band nearly split up and the album *Thirteen* was a huge disappointment. Tons of money was spent. Although the songs were good, it was a real fuck up. And this is the joke: *Bandwagonesque* we had fuck all to do with it and when you're successful and you've got fuck all to do with it you should just leave it alone. The manager, Chas, demanded that we go up on these sojourns to fucking Manchester to get involved. So it was the only Teenage Fanclub album we've ever really been involved with. So we all went up every two weeks. And what happens? Nothing fucking happened. The record they made sold 150,000 copies round the world which they now have sold every other album since then. On this new album there's a tune where I said, 'If you change the bottom end of that and put a hip-hop beat under it, it's a fucking hit. I'll get Youth to do something'. And they go, 'Oh, join the queue'. And I went, 'No, you don't understand. He's one of my wife's mates.' So I phoned up Youth and went, 'What do you reckon of Teenage Fanclub?' He replied, 'I fucking love them'. And I said, 'What are you doing?' And he went, 'Oh, I'm just changing nappies, but I could do with a bit of rock 'n' roll, send me it.' So I send him it. 'Tell you what,' he goes, 'I'll do it but I need to re-record it, Alan, because I need to get them into the groove of what I want to do. We'll put Will Malone's strings on it and we'll really build it towards the choruses.' This is the guy that conceptualised 'Bitter Sweet Symphony' and other amazing fucking records; he's a genius producer who Oasis should have used on the last album. I always wanted Youth because I thought Noel should have been working with somebody that has a genius in music. But anyway, I phoned up the band and said, 'Youth will do it but he wants to re-record'. 'Okay let's think about it,' was the answer they gave me. And the next day they said, 'No, it's either a remix or we're not re-recording it'. So you've got to ask yourself a question. One of the top producers in the world wants to record your track and thinks it's a hit and is prepared to do it and you don't want him to do it.

So what is that actually saying? I think that's saying I think we're happy with 150,000 sales, ultimately.

CHAPTER FIVE

KLE: At that time I was still involved a bit in the production side of things and because I didn't know Kevin Shields I tried to keep as professional a relationship as I could with him. I do remember going over to the studio to show him a promo of the album *Loveless* and him not liking it because he wanted the whole thing to be red and there were certain things that looked pink. It all needed to be different shades of red. I suppose tensions were high but you know there were times too when there would just be a big joke made out of it. How many years does it take to get an album out of them, and that kinda stuff.

LAURENCE: Alan was really upset with them and there was a very bad vibe at Creation and I was caught in the middle because I had to make the most of my press campaign. I had hostility on both sides. When I was asking Creation to give me the cash I needed because I had to take Danny Kelly to this that and the other thing – to get them to agree was difficult. On the band's side there was a lot of suspicion. I am very proud of what I did on *Loveless*, actually. But I can only do a good job if I like the record I am working on.

ED BALL: I think Alan was very stressed out. Dick was pretty stressed out. They used to take it in turns to call up the Valentines and have a daily 'What's going on? What's happening?' session. Dick, perhaps, was closer to them because they were a drinking band and a band that he kind of really got on well with.

K: People saw Alan and Dick's relationship with the Valentines as a good cop–bad cop thing. Dick's just always standing there behind Alan and holding onto the purse strings.

SIMON STEPHENS: Dick was the backbone of it all and he kept it all together. He was like the Head schoolteacher and Alan owned the school. Dick used to crack the whip and say, 'Enough is enough and we'll get on with the real business of selling records.'

L: I think at some point Alan thought whatever Creation touched was going to turn into a massive success.

K: I used to do the meetings at Creation in the Hackney days. I'd have to turn my computer off halfway through because it would just all of a sudden be Lawrence talking about who she saw down the Underworld and it would just turn into a gossip-fest, to the extent that we'd have to say, 'Okay let's get back to the next band that we have to talk about.' We'd always go off onto a tangent and in a way it was a bit of a time waster. But everyone was so together then. It was so great, whereas now it's all: stick to the like point one, point two, point three, and everyone would leave thinking 'Okay, this is my job and I've got to do this this and that, and he's got to that, and I'm going to make sure he does it. Whatever.'
In the old days everyone did their job no matter how messed up they were from the night before. They always showed up. Maybe a bit late, but everyone always did their job and people always stayed late without it being a problem. When we moved to Primrose Hill that stopped happening,

JOE FOSTER: About '90 –'91, I started to come back to myself and almost out of all the big boozes and I went back to Creation and started doing re-issues and things. That was quite good, put out loads of old records. William Shatner and all that kind of stuff. Fred Neil, he's still sending me Christmas cards!

EB: Dick used to embarrass me because he was working so hard and I really endeavoured to be more like him. I wish I could have been. I really wish I could have concentrated more and made more. I always hoped that I could be more diligent. Speak with

THE CHAPS!

OASIS 2000

ROCK 'N' ROLL STARS!

ALAN – THE ECSTASY YEARS, '88

TOP: THE PRIORY TABLE . . . FROM THE LEFT TRASHMONK, ALAN, PATSY, LIAM, JAMES BROWN AND KAZ BROWN AT BRIX SMITH'S WEDDING.

BELOW: KATE, ALLY McCOIST, ALAN, AND TREVOR STEVENS AT T IN THE PARK, '95

**KING KEVIN – THE GREATEST
SOUL SINGER IN THE WORLD!**

1O DOWNING STREET
LONDON SW1A 2AA

From the Chief Press Secretary   2 March 2000

<u>Personal</u>

[handwritten greeting]

    Having read your *Express* interview, I'm sorry that you feel the way you do, but I really believe you overlook the scale of the anti-poverty agenda the Government is pushing through. I really don't think the Henley-on-Thames line is sustainable. The Government is doing a lot for Springburn and Moss Side, but some of the problems there are going to take years to sort. But I think if you look at what we are trying to do, I hope you'll see our heart remains in the right place, and that we are making a difference.

    As Tony has said, <u>we</u> want things to happen quicker, but they <u>are</u> happening, as I hope you'll see if you take a look at the speech he gave on Sunday, a copy of which I enclose.

    I hear what you say about Millbank and, if someone said you were "ill" in the way suggested, that is wrong. But again, you know as well as I do that the press will use anything to do us in, and my understanding is that a party press officer, asked by *The Sun* where they could get hold of you, said you had not been well (i.e. had got flu or some such). I don't know the full story there, but I do know I don't take the press's word at face value, and I also know that the reason I'm still at it round the clock is because I believe we are delivering, step by step, for the people and the social justice causes you and I believe in.

[handwritten signature]

ALASTAIR CAMPBELL

Alan McGee

'POLITICS? I WOULD RATHER GIVE MY MONEY TO CHARITY' – ALAN McGEE AUGUST 2000

ALAN '97. 'OFF THE SNIFF'

some of the bands and some of them will say, 'Oh that fucking bald cunt! I mean the number of things he fucked up for us.' And I'm sorry. Yes, it's true. It's true.

JF: With the Sony deal, initially it seemed very hopeful that we'd have the finance and access to all kinds of things. It kind of worked for a bit but it just took a turn downhill. Basically, we started getting marketing people in who thought it was their label and I thought they seemed totally deluded. It's like me going to work for the BBC and thinking it's my radio station. Working for Alan McGee no matter how much you do or how much you think of yourself, it's his label – not your label. And they didn't seem to get it. And I could see Alan would eventually get pissed off with it, but I just didn't know how long or what form it would take. So, it just got really weird, a lot of bands went, people we'd had for years who had their own wee cult. Ed Ball and the Jazz Butcher were pushed off the planet and I think Alan possibly started to get quite annoyed when they got rid of the Jasmines. It was like a step too fucking far. Their point of view was just as deluded as somebody in a band that's got some mad idea that bears no relation to reality and decides to follow it. To me the way they acted was the way Kevin Shields acted when he was really chasing something that he couldn't define, and spending tons of money on it. To me it was exactly similar this kind of behaviour: it was just completely deluded, spending a vast amount of money selling something that no-one's interested in. Just like there would be no attention for certain things that we had.

SS: McGee used to sign things to wind people up. He knew that Swervedriver would wind people up. He probably thought, 'Well if I got Swervedriver in the office, and Bobby Gillespie and Stephens or someone like that's about, I know it's gonna wind them up, and at some point they're gonna say something.'

SUSAN McGEE: Sony had their own people watching over and so I think that probably ruined it because it wasn't just his baby any more, it was Sony and they had accountants and they want to know where money is being spent and Alan, of course, is spending it all over the shop. The freedom thing must have went big time.

K: At the beginning it was intimidating because he was my boss and I didn't know him and I was really struggling to understand what he said a lot of the times. And I was obviously really aware that he was moody, and now looking back on it I see it was his drug personality. I became his PA, and also I started doing production helping getting label copy and stuff together for all the albums. I was just really into the music and thought this is the atmosphere I want to be in, Alan would ring up and I'm a little superstitious – I would knock wood every single time he was paged through to me. 'Its Alan on the phone.' 'Okay'. [she knocks twice on the table] and then I'd pick it up and be like, 'Please God let him be in a good mood today.'

If he was in a good mood he'd launch into it, 'You wouldn't believe who was in the hot tub last night, this that and the other!' You'd get the gossip and it was always good. And if he was in a bad mood he'd be like, 'Where are my press department? Nobody's in press, call so and so at home, give her an ultimatum. It's my record company.' He'd say that a lot, 'It's my record company.' When he was in a good mood there was nothing like it. He was so much fun. And there's something that he's naturally got to his personality which is so inspiring.

EB: Sometimes he would say, 'I'm gonna knock it all on the head, I'm gonna stop doing this, I'm gonna stop doing the drink and drugs.' Everybody does. I thought, 'He'll be alright.' And then he'd start up again. There'd be another trip somewhere. Or he'd be off somewhere with Tim Abbot.

SM: He bumped into Keith Richards in the lift in Los Angeles. They had just taken a big massive line of coke and just as the coke was reaching its peak the doors of the lift opened and Keith Richards is standing there. And they all went, 'For fuck sake!'

SS: He really loved Belinda. He loved her as much as I loved my Swedish bird. He was the ginger-haired Scotsman that couldn't fucking pull a bird; I was like the working-class loudmouth that couldn't pull a decent bird. Then all of sudden you've got this beautiful Swedish chick and you've got Belinda. All my mates used to fancy her to fuck. I'd be like, 'No, no, that's the boss's bird.'

Alan said to me once, 'You know what Simon? These ecstasy romances they're never gonna last.' And he was right. I was in one and he was in one. He probably won't remember it but he did say it. He was probably telling me not to kid myself because when you're doing E you are loved up, you are full on love induced and everything's great.

EB: Drugs would change everyone's perception of time. Time would metamorphose into one long afternoon. And this is like weekdays sort of thing. Obviously the label had started to expand and they started to put a few people in to come and run certain things like the distribution and the accounts. So the straight people who'd been brought in to do specific jobs found it a bit hard going when there was someone from one of the bands lying on their desk, you know, off their head. So it was a clash of cultures. Definitely, a clash of cultures.

K: I liked the way something could just explode all of a sudden. I remember one time we booked a Creation Christmas party at that place where there is a Chinese Elvis and he sings Elvis songs and everyone sits around and has this big Chinese meal. And we booked a table for 25 people at this restaurant for our Christmas party. I'd gone home and was getting ready to meet everybody there, but they all stayed in the office. Mistake. I remember Christine Wanless ringing me up at about nine o' clock saying 'Kle we are all too fucked to go to this party, can you please call and cancel it because we're in too much of a mess,' and me having to ring up this restaurant and cancel this booking that was in an hour's time for 25 people. But everything was always very spontaneous.

SS: It all gelled, it all worked, so it's basically down to respect, but I think Alan would be the first to admit that he lost his self-respect when he got into, you know, the partying and then the breakdown.

MARK GARDNER: Things were beginning to get a bit out of hand for Alan. I could just see that his stress levels were going up and I remember saying to him, 'Actually, Alan, I think that you need to go away for a bit or just chill out because it's all getting a bit much.'

SUSAN McGEE

PAOLO HEWITT: WE SHOULD TALK ABOUT THE NIGHT ALAN SIGNED OASIS BECAUSE YOU WERE THERE AS WELL, WEREN'T YOU?

SUSAN McGEE: That's right, yeah.

PH: And is it true that Alan went there because you had a mate that he wanted to hook up with?

SM: Aye.

PH: Who was it, what was the girl's name?

SM: Annette. It's funny. She didn't know anything of it. And we were just sort of sitting there and it was me and Alan and my ex-boyfriend. And we'd been up in Alan's hotel room getting absolutely . . . we were just drinking bottles of [Mobile phone rings, stops to answer]. What were we talking about? Oh, aye, the Oasis night.

PH: You were tanked up and . . . ?

SM: Uh huh. We went down really early. I think because my watch was wrong. I can't remember.

PH: Alan said it was because you didn't realise that the pub had an extension. He said if he had realised the pub had an extension, you'd have got there for 10 p.m.

SM: Well, we went down. It was about 8 p.m. or something and we just walked in. We were sitting there and there were all these like guys that looked like Mods – not like your typical kind of Glasgow. They were all pretty lairy and this guy Tam Coyle – the guy that runs and puts the bands on – came up to Alan and said, 'Listen. There is a band that are totally wanting to play and if they don't play they are gonna batter everybody backstage.' And Alan went, 'What are you telling me for? Just let them play. What harm can it do?'

PH: SISTER LOVER USED TO REHEARSE IN THE SAME ROOM AS OASIS IN MANCHESTER. IS THIS HOW THEY KNEW ABOUT THIS GIG?

SM: Is that what it was? My pal actually told me he was there and he can't remember being there because he was so drunk. That would really piss you off. But they were amazing. You were just like, 'Bloody Hell!' I said, 'Alan, you've got to sign them.' And he was saying, 'I know. I know.'

Later, Alan just went straight up to Noel and he asked who their manager was or something and basically said, 'Listen. I'm really interested.' I mean, it was amazing. Never seen anything like that. Liam just had a presence. And there was only about 12 people watching. Bizarre.

PH: There's film of it you know?

SM: Aye. A Japanese girl's got it, I know.

PH: Amazing isn't it? Some night.

SM: Totally.

PH: And did you go back to the hotel with Alan?

SM: No. I started a new job the next day and so I had to go back.

PH: And did he get off with Annette?

SM: No. She got married.

Oasis? I think that it was just perfect, that it was a great moment in time. If there had been another record company at that same gig they'd have all walked out. And I really believe that. I don't think that anybody else would have got it, believed in it, shouted about it. I mean he knew straight away and that's Alan McGee.

Jeff Barrett

ALAN McGEE

ALAN McGEE: It's a complete fluke that I did find them. I was up seeing my own band 18 Wheeler. My mate Debbie Turner's band was playing the same night. And I just thought, 'I've got to go for a laugh. It's her first ever gig. She'll be totally freaked out.' I was in Glasgow. My band's playing. So I'll go and check out 18 Wheeler play live.

PH: DIDN'T YOUR SISTER GO TO THE GIG WITH A GIRL THAT YOU WANTED TO MEET?

AM: Yeah, yeah, that was true as well, aye. I was there to see if 18 Wheeler could play live and there to freak Debbie out. There was a late licence going on in Glasgow and I got there at 8 p.m. and the first band wasn't on till half past ten. So I had two hours to drink Jack Daniels and Coke. In the meantime there was this guy that was in this other band, Boyfriend, that Dave Barker signed to August Records, which was a subsidiary of ours at the time. He came up to me and said. 'McGee, it's gonna go off, it's gonna go off. Debbie's brought her mates up and they can't play and the bouncers are gonna have it with them and they're gonna have it with the bouncers.' I replied, 'What are they called?'. And he said, 'Oasis. They're a fucking bunch of scallies, there's about fifteen of them and there's only about two bouncers.' And I went, 'Go and say to the bouncers, let them play for four songs,' because I had Boyfriend and 18 Wheeler playing. So it was our night, ultimately. I added my weight to make it kind of hard for them not to get a gig. And I think if they hadn't got a gig I think Oasis probably would have smashed up the bar. So anyway, they got allowed to do it. It was pure Oasis. They were raising the roof of King Tut's.

And this is the first time I saw Liam Gallagher. And you turned around and you clocked this guy – this is before sportswear was fucking trendy – and he's sitting in Adidas like a young Weller, right, and you just went, 'Geezer. You are fucking cool.' But I thought he was a drug dealer and the guy that's going to sing is probably going to be a fucking bricklayer going bald. He had blue Adidas tracksuit bottoms on. They got on stage and Liam had a lot of presence, only we'd seen it before and it was called Ian Brown. Anyway, the band was fucking unbelievable. I was a reasonably shite guitar player but tuned in enough to always spot a great guitar player. So it got to the guitar solo. Usually the making or breaking of a guitar band is, can the lead guy cut it? And I was like, 'Okay, the song's pretty good up until now. The singer's got charisma – can the guitarist . . . ' The guitar solo was great. It was 'Bring It On Down'. And I was like, 'Fuck.' And I said to Susan, 'This is really good.' You know, I had a shock. And then they went into 'Up In The Sky' and the solo again was fucking unbelievable.

'I'm gonna sign them.' I said. They did one other song and then they did the Beatles song 'I Am The Walrus', which is so hard to do it so fucking well. I thought, being a total opportunist, I thought, 'The Stone Roses haven't had a record out for three or four years so I can nip in before the Stone Roses get theirs out, stick it out as I did with Ride and My Bloody Valentine, to other Stone Roses fans. If I get it right I might sell as many as the Stone Roses and sell half a million copies. And in the back of my head I thought, 'I might be able to bail myself out of that fucking debacle that's called Primal Scream going on in my back yard' right. But that was it. It was never like, you know, 'Is Noel Gallagher gonna have a house in Chalfont St. Giles with 20 million under his bed?' It was never that one. It was like, 'Fucking hell, maybe I can fucking offset the Primal Scream heroin debacle with fucking Oasis and live to tell the tale.'

So then I went up to Mark Coyle. I knew Coyley because he had got sacked by Teenage Fanclub, and said, 'Who's the leader of the group?'. And he went, 'The guitar player.' 'Tell them that I'm interested.' And he went, 'I'll go and get them. Tell them yourself'. So Noel Gallagher comes and I said, 'Do you want a record deal? I thought it was fucking amazing.' And he said, 'Well I'll get you a demo tape'. I said, 'I don't think I need a tape. I think I know that you're good enough on that.' And he went, 'No, I'll get you a tape and see if you like it.' I went back to this hotel, the Lorne Park, and phoned up Abbot and Dick and Johnny and Bobby and I said, 'I might be wrong but I think I've fucking found this fucking amazing band.' Then I came back and got in the office and then Noel, Bonehead and Liam came on down and met me, Abbot and Dick.

This is pure Noel Gallagher. This is one of the few things I wish he had never told me later but it actually says quite a lot about his character. In Hackney we had a room we called the Bunker. It was like Hitler's bunker right. You came down the stairs like that and a whole wall was pictures of supermodels. My girlfriend at the time said it was the most sexist thing she had ever seen in her life. You'd walk in and it was just pictures of Kate Moss, Linda Evangelista, Claudia Schiffer on the whole wall. And then on another wall there were just pictures of people who had been blown up and bombed and stuff like that. It was just our sense of humour. So you had models there. You had loads of people on another wall that had been blown up.

Down the stairs, Blu-Tacked to the fucking wall was Rod Stewart, Marvin Gaye, Johnny Rotten, Paul Simenon and all my heroes. Noel being Noel gets into the building and he's clocking pictures of Paul Simenon, Rod Stewart, Alex Chilton and so on. So he sits down. Bonehead's in the middle. Liam's there. Abbot sits at the end of the desk. I go, like, 'What music are you into?' Noel said 'Rod fucking Stewart. I said 'Fucking Rod Stewart. Amazing man.' And then he'd go, 'Paul Simenon, coolest fucking bass player in the world.' And I said 'Fucking Paul Simenon. Fucking Amazing.' I think we got to Little Feat and he blagged Little Feat as well! By the end of it I was going, 'Fucking Soul Brother Man!' The only other person that I have ever totally connected with over music is Gillespie. I said, 'We're doing whatever it takes, we are doing the deal with you.' He went, 'Right, shake on it because everybody's always let me down in the music business. Do you mean it?'. And I went, 'It's a fucking done deal.'

PH: BUT THE ONE THING ABOUT THAT DEAL WAS THAT, IF I'M NOT MISTAKEN, THEY WANTED YOU TO CHANGE YOUR LICENSEES ABROAD BECAUSE THEY DIDN'T LIKE THE MAN IN AMERICA DID THEY?

AM: They took a trip to America to meet different people and . . .

PH: Noel and Marcus went and they met your American licensee. He listened to the demo, turned to them and said, 'You're from Manchester. You're like Jesus Jones, right?'

AM: Yeah. And I think that was the definite turning point. Because at one point we felt as if we were never gonna get the deal. And then it came up. 'We want to sign to Epic and we want to sign to you.' And so eventually it ended up, 'Tell you what, we'll sign to Epic in America and you can give them the UK licence'. And that's how it kind of happened.

PH: WAS THERE A LOT OF PARTYING WITH OASIS?

AM: I think that was part of my decline. Not to blame them but I think that was a big part of the decline of me. Basically, my girlfriend had lived with me between '88 and '92 . . .

PH: This is Belinda?

AM: Yeah. She had a set of her own problems and she went home. I had this on-off relationship. I was out with the Scream, even though aesthetically, we were probably all drifting apart. I really thought that Bob was drifting into being some sort of rock star that I couldn't really relate to but the drugs were kind of tying us together. And then if I wasn't partying with the Scream then I was just basically trying to like shag like anything that was available and female.

And so there was a lot of partying with girls and stuff like that. Then Oasis came along. And then it kind of went up 50% again. It was like, 'Fuck, it can't get any more.' There was hardly ever a night off and I'd started really getting into things like diet pills and stuff like that because I was a porky fucker. I wanted to be skinny but I was drinking like fuck. So I was like, I was just doing drugs, coke, fucking E, Jack Daniels, but I was also doing diet pills. And they are just like the cheapest shit of speed you could ever fucking take. And although it was a party, and yeah I was getting plenty of sex, I was actually really miserable because deep down I just wanted to be with my girlfriend who was really tired and drifting out of the relationship more and more. I think I was too much for her to be honest. I was mission impossible.

PH: YOU ARE AT ROTHERHITHE AT THIS POINT? AND YOU HAD A JACUZZI THERE?

AM: Yeah, yeah. Jacuzzi in the basement and all that gear. And Oasis upped the ante. Not only did I have the Primals but I had Oasis. And the Gallaghers were like hardcore. Noel more than Liam at this point. He was much more serious about it. Liam was like just a kid. He was 21. Noel used to say that Liam was baffled by me and the drummer, Tony McCarroll, was just scared by me. And then Bonehead and Guigs, I don't think anything could really scare these two fuckers. They had seen a lot more hardcore drug taking than me I think.

PH: Noel had moved to London hadn't he . . .

AM: No. Not at that point. He was down a lot but he was breaking up with Louise, his girlfriend. And he was living between the two places. But he was desperate to move on. It was as if the minute Oasis really started he had written off Manchester and wanted to move out of it immediately. Whatever, he was running fast. I mean probably the fondest period I have ever had with Noel Gallagher was '93 into '94. That's the last time I was close to Noel. But that first year-and-a-half I was pretty close with him. Me and Abbot spent a lot of time in the studio before I finally flipped my lid. They went to Wales and they never really worked. I listened to it and it was scrapped. We scrapped 50 grand of the recording costs and then we started again. We were doing it at Olympia and we had 'Bring It On Down'. I wanted to come out with that single because it was so in your face and fuck you. Me and Noel thought 'That's the first single' but we had 'Supersonic' as a demo. 'Supersonic' was a fucking demo! I remember sitting down and I'd come down with like four or five gram and I was chopping them out and turning around to Noel, charlie'd off my head, I went, 'What do you reckon?' And he just went, 'Let's fucking put it out.' And that was the start. You see it always goes back to Punk rock for me. I got criticised by Ian Brown in one of the Sunday papers about a year ago when he said, 'The problem with McGee is he's never got over punk rock.' I'd say that was my asset not my fucking failing. But the guy is right: I've never got over Punk rock.

ALAN McGEE

AM: The Primals are probably the best band in the world. Definitely the best ever band on Creation. You've got to understand their relationship with me. Bobby was on the label because he was my mate. It's like I love Ed Ball's music you know. Is Ed Ball ever going to sell a load of records? Probably not. He's never had a hit in his life, right, but he's on the label because he's my friend and I believe in him and Gillespie. After six years they suddenly had a hit record and I was in shock, man. But having said that now I'm working the way right through all the different records and coming up to *Xtrmntr* they are the greatest. I mean, bands have their moments. Like you, I know you're gonna agree with me, it's like the Stone Roses had their moment or The Jam had their moment right. Probably, the ultimate Jam moment was the fifth album. What was that called?

PH: *Sound Affects?*

AM: *Sound Affects.* To me that's probably The Jam moment right. And Joy Division had their moment. And like My Bloody Valentine had their moment. And everybody had their moment. And I'd say if Oasis had their moment it was '94–'96. Primal Scream's moment is now. Unbelievably, a bunch of 40-year-old blokes are pushing the envelope further than any anybody else. But this is their moment now. I believe in them more now than I did fucking 15 years ago.

PH: DO YOU BELIEVE IN THEM AS PEOPLE?

AM: I always believed in them as people. Always. That's what I always believed in. I always thought that there was something genius about them as human beings.

PH: Because the thing that really took me about them, apart from their talent as a live band because that's where I think they shine, was their gang mentality.

AM: Totally. They have still got that.

PH: And they just fitted in so well with each other.

AM: I suppose Primal Scream is a gang of outsiders. So that's kind of weird in itself. So maybe they have taken it to its most logical conclusion. But then again you know, I used to be part of *the* gang and now I'm not. You know what I mean. I am now not part of the gang because I don't indulge the way that they still indulge, but you know I find the Primal Scream gang mentality kind of weird. I don't particularly understand how that can be attractive to somebody of 39 years of age. But having said that, it is up to them. They all get off on it. And maybe they get off on it because they back each other up and it's a belief system that Andrew and Bobby and Robert and Mani all believe in. Maybe it's like that. But I'm much more of an outsider in life. I mean I'm prepared to be outside everything, you know what I mean? But it works for them. I mean, fuck man, it's like they're defying fucking gravity. To be 39 and to be cutting edge, it's unbelievable you know. I mean I think they are as important a band as Joy Division or something like that now, you know what I mean? And I think *Xtrmntr* with a bit of luck might sell a million records around the world right. I think it's about 300,000 at the moment. It's going to be one of the great albums of this year. Top-three album. Maybe Album of the Year. You'll find in ten years time when people look back at, you know, at this period, I think people will say, 'Primal Scream were one of *the* bands.'

PH: AND THEY CAME FROM NOWHERE AS WELL, TO DO IT, DIDN'T THEY?

AM: Yeah. Completely.

PH: From the brink of nowhere really.

AM: They lost the plot, I mean as much as I lost the plot in a drug way, I think they lost the plot in a drug way but it wasn't just focused on one individual. Bobby had depression through using too much Temazepan. And I think Innes never really got to the brink other than his dabblings with heroin in '92. But Throb definitely has been to hell and back, man. I mean if you could get Throb to talk Paolo, that's a book. That band have been right over the edge and come back. And I think *Vanishing Point* was a return to form and then *Xtrmntr* invented a new sound. And I think the way that people revere the Velvets and revere a lot of those bands, I think it's gonna be a one of them, one of those records, this record. It's gonna be a seminal sort of release.

PH: HOW LONG DID *SCREAMADELICA* TAKE TO COME TOGETHER?

AM: Probably about a year and a half but there was so much drug taking and partying. It was spread out. Then Throb would phone me up and say, 'I've heard this amazing remix. Hire Steve Anderson to do a remix'. I would spend £5,000 and this guy sent something back that was like Italian stadium house. This is not Primal Scream. Then I found out he'd got the wrong Anderson. It would be Paul Anderson.

PH: And you yourself had to come back as well.

AM: At the end of the day I had a nervous breakdown. We went through bad times, with money. My relationship was on the rocks. Belinda was partying really hard with the drugs and stuff like that, so I was struggling with all that bullshit. But the bottom line is, not only was it a party with the Primals but the Gallaghers had come along. And every time they were in London it was like going out for two days solid. Not only did I have one load of people that were insane, I had another couple of people that were absolutely insane. And so you were doubling it up. And then I was the one that had to work the party because I was the figurehead and I was the party animal. I was the one that was supposed to be still keeping the business together and having hits. And I just fucking went off my tits!

JEFF BARRETT

JEFF BARRETT: Out of the blue McGee rang me up and said 'Barrett I need to meet you.' This is way down the line and we weren't close at all. Hardly saw each other. So I met him in this pub and he said 'I really want you to do the press on the Scream.' The album I started working on was the *Give Out But Don't Give Up* album, so that would be pre '94. My label, Heavenly, had just been dropped by Sony and I had learnt an awful lot. Actually, I was hurting so the timing was so brilliant for me because I'd been dropped and I needed some time to work out if I'd failed. What had I done wrong? Am I crap? Can I actually do this? It kept me focused, it gave me an income, it gave me two years to focus on one group and also work out what had happened with my Sony relationship, so it was great. Two weeks later I flew to Memphis, told them what time I was arriving, turned up at the studio, no band. The first person I met is Tom Dowd who I knew by reputation and legend. The Primals turned up several hours later after a trip to New Orleans.

PAOLO HEWITT: WHAT DID YOU THINK OF THE ALBUM?
JB: It was a peculiar record, some of it was really good, some of it wasn't and I turned it into one of my best jobs and got a lot of press. Yeah I did blag it a bit but I believed in that band so I wasn't lying too much, I didn't ever have to lie. I'd been a bit low profile on the press side of things so it was nice for me to go into these offices and play it. It was the best press they ever had on that album weirdly enough. It sold as well. So it was me back on board with them. It was odd because Alan was really distant then, really distant.

I remember being in a hotel room with George Clinton and Bobby Gillespie in New York and staying in this hotel that looks over the big Cathedral. It was like Gotham City. And they'd ended this interview and I remember Alan ringing, and him and Bob kind of talking and being odd. Neither of them really knew what to say. Bob was lost, Innes was *totally* lost, Alan was breaking down, they were all fucking breaking down and I think if you've been friends with someone for such a long time, how weird it is for both sides? Alan started blaming them for things, they had to deal with that as well. It was really horrible. He was ill. The doctors could tell us that . . . But while everybody was curled up at home listening to *Screamadelica*, they were sat there at home listening to Freddie Scott, Otis Clay, which is why they went to Memphis to make the record. Good move? Bad move? Who gives a shit. This was a Primal Scream move. This is what they did, it's not up to anybody outside of that group to say that was a dumb move, which is why I did that job. I didn't care what these people had to say, I had to just go in there and make sure this record didn't get lost. Simple as that. I couldn't allow people to give that record bad reviews and if they were going to give it bad reviews, I had to make sure they were on the front covers before the bad press hit.

ALAN McGEE

PAOLO HEWITT: YOU HAD JUST SIGNED TO SONY AND YOUR LAST QUOTE WAS, 'THAT'S WHERE IT ALL WENT WRONG'.

AM: I think that was probably the beginning of it starting to go wrong. Everything ends up really environmental. You know, if you go and live in a country environment then you end up talking to a lot of farmers rather than other kinds of people. If you end up having to talk to a lot of corporate people you end up becoming corrupted by that mentality.

PH: GIVE ME AN EXAMPLE OF THAT.

AM: Instead of people raving, 'Have you heard that Teenage Fanclub album? Have you heard that My Bloody Valentine album?' It's 'Have you got a hit band?' Primal Scream were the flagship band and when they never happened there was a lot of pressure on us by '94 to come out with something that was really special. And it was lucky that we ran into Oasis because really the label would have crashed on the rocks by '94.

I mean it went down after *Give Out But Don't Give Up* because the recording costs on that album were the most expensive recording costs I've ever incurred in 17 years in the music business right. You could buy two recording studios with the amount of money that they spent. £420,000 and we had no hits. We had Tom Dowd who had been mixing it and everything sounded flat. And we sent it to George Drakoulias. I wanted him from the beginning and they did not want to use him because he'd done the Black Crowes. Which I find kind of vaguely ironic considering that we had songs like 'Rocks' on it and both bands were nicking off the Rolling Stones. I just thought, 'Why don't we just give it to George who can deliver this kind of music?' Innes went over to Los Angeles and I got a phone call during the night and it was Drakoulias. And he played 'Rocks' down my phone and I put it on speakerphone and he had put this glam rock sample drum right through it and it just sounded amazing. And then I thought, 'Well at least we are gonna get our money back.' But that album ended up costing £420,000. The marketing of that album was probably about another half a million. So there was a million riding on that album right. And it was basically a little label. Still only about 25 people at the time.

So it was a million pounds, which was a lot of money. It came out and was met with complete disgruntlement by people because it was over produced, as it would be if you spend £420,000 on an album. Nobody really wanted it. Even though you've got to say that 'Rocks' is an amazing sound and 'Cry Myself Blind' is a great track as well. But that was the spin on that. So really we were gonna crash and the thing that kept us alive through that was Oasis coming out the traps with 'Supersonic'. Sony smelt it and said, 'Wait a minute, we might have just got a superstar'.

PH: This seems to be a somewhat unhealthy period for the Primals.

AM: Well, the thing is, the first Primal Scream period really was '84–'87. And then '87 to '88 were the speed years. By '89 they had discovered ecstasy. And that was it really. And then by about '90 there was individuals starting to dabble with the brown.

And then by about '92 going in to '93 the manager was addicted to heroin, the producer was addicted to heroin and the three of the band were addicted to heroin. So that was like, that was basically like as black as you are ever gonna get in any situation, do you know what I mean?

PH: AND HOW WAS YOUR RELATIONSHIP WITH THEM AT THIS JUNCTURE?

AM: It was starting to deteriorate. I stopped managing them March '92 because it was a conflict of interest and it was quite hard for me to give that up because I'd been managing them since '84. I'd got them to 500,000 sales. I'd broke the band. They were playing Brixton Academy. They were happening. We were the hippest fucking thing in the world at that point. But I knew I had to give the management away. I never took a commission but I got 50% of the records and they got 50% of the records, it was a real kind of bond thing that we were working on.

But once they started getting seriously into drugs and once they got a bit of freedom they started slowly *buying into* the myth. I mean Bob never said that he wasn't going to buy into the myth. I think my relationship with him started going weird after *Screamadelica*. And one of the reasons I gave in management of the band was I remember Bob phoning up, obviously off his nut on drugs, and going mad at me because the roadies hadn't been paid and it was about three days after the tour or something like that. And I'm just thinking, 'I'm not even getting paid for this,' I mean, what other record company guy manages the band for no money. See, we'd been grooming Alex Nightingale even though he was an out-and-out fucking drug fiend at that point. He was a good guy and he was an honest guy and he was our guy really more than anything, right.

PH: HOW DID YOU KNOW ALEX?

AM: Just met him in a club in Brighton in '89 and got him a job in the music business.

PH: You seem to do this all the time, give out jobs to people who have never done that type of work.

AM: Yeah well what happens, we were in this club and it was about five minutes before the end of the night and I went, 'I need an E.' I knew Nightingale was Annie's son, but I barely knew him. I went up to him about mid-way through '89 and I went 'Can you get us an E?' And he went, 'Are you McGee from Creation?' So he went and he got me two E. I went, 'How much?' And he went, 'Oh, get the money for tomorrow; call it credit.' So then we went back to my place in Brighton that was above Bobby Gillespie's. There was me, Nightingale and this guy called James Williamson. We just started having a mad party and it was kind of mental. It was a bit like the Red Hot Chilli Peppers on drugs or something; firing CDs at each other and hitting each other on the head. It was a bit bizarre.

And then in the morning I got up and Nightingale was still there. And he says, 'Oh fuck I'd better go. I've got to phone this guy about a job.' 'What's the guy's name?' I said. And he replies 'Mike Hine.' And I went, 'That's one of my pals.' And he goes, 'I've been trying to get in the music business for about a year and a half but people won't employ me because I'm Annie Nightingale's son and they think it's nepotism.' So I phoned Hine up and I went, 'Look, my pal is coming to see you, give him a job.' And he went, 'Yeah just send him up as long as he's not a fucking drug addict he'll be fine' I went, [laughing] 'I'll send him up anyway.' So it was like, that's how we met Nightingale. Nightingale became the agent within six months. So then at Brixton Academy, I sort of handed the management of the band over to Alex. I think they did three shows that March and I gave Nightingale the management of the band.

PH: BUT THE PRIMALS WERE KEEPING YOU GOING?
AM: Not really. I mean, to be absolutely honest Sony kept us going. And the other thing that kept us going was me going off and doing these deals like selling the rights to American record companies. Primal Scream never lost us money, to their credit, and might have made us a bit of money, but they never kept the operation going. My scamming, going off and taking lots of money out of other record companies, that's what really was keeping us going. But to look at their egos which were such that you thought they were selling 40 million records: when in reality they were selling 500,000. But then the Indie scene hadn't exploded. 'Morning Glory', Blur and Pulp hadn't come through yet.

PH: DID YOU HAVE MUCH TO DO WITH THE MAKING OF 'GIVE OUT'?
AM: I went down about three times to the Roundhouse and it was called the 'Brownhouse'. You would go down to the studio and you would see them watching the same programme at 3 p.m. gouching out. And after the third time, because I'd never really been into smack, it was hard for me to really spot it. It took me a bit of time to tune in to what was really going on. And then I twigged that, 'Wait a minute. The

drugs have moved on here. It is not coke any more, it is not fucking E, it is not acid, it is not speed. This is *smack*.'

PH: HOW LONG WERE THEY AT THE ROUNDHOUSE FOR?
AM: Six weeks to two months.

PH: TO DO WHAT? JUST START THE ALBUM?
AM: To start the album. I've got 40 hours of them doing cover versions. If the plane ever goes down they've got the box set! Unfortunately it was only about five songs they ever covered. It was very messy. But when they went to Memphis they were going to get away from Camden and drugs really. That's why they went to Memphis. Of course, when I went out there we're all doing humungous amounts of cocaine but at the end of the day it wasn't smack. And the two guys that did come off the shit basically did so by drinking their way down off it.

PH: HOW LONG ARE THEY OUT IN MEMPHIS FOR?
AM: Three months.
PH: And did it work with Tom Dowd? Did they respect him?
AM: They did. I think it was old school tactics. It was, 'Bobby, you've got to get a singing teacher' – not that Bob ever did get a singing teacher – 'And every word has got to be in tune.' Whereas I think Bob's now accepted that he's not gonna be the greatest singer ever.
PH: But after that album, Bobby doesn't sing on anything for about three years. I remember reading this article in *Mojo* by Tom Dowd.
AM: And he put him down?
PH: He really put him down.
AM: I mean Tom Dowd, he was a good producer but at the end of the day I rejected the mixes, so Tom Dowd can think what he likes but his mixes got rejected by the record company.
PH: So you'd spent all this money on the album and it hadn't taken off.
AM: Yeah, yeah.
PH: Which is when you go into rehab.
AM: Right.

SUSAN McGEE

PAOLO HEWITT: WHEN THIS E THING HAPPENED AND ALL THAT YOU MUST HAVE BEEN HIDING ALL THIS FROM YOUR PARENTS?

SUSAN McGEE: Well my mum was dead by then. But one time when Alan was up for the weekend we had a party that just went wrong. We heard the doorbell, and I was like that, 'Listen, that's the door, fling the bag over there.' And I answered the door and my dad just took one look and just walked away. Just left. I came back in the room and I went, 'Alan. Dad,' and I threw my arms round him, going 'Oh shit.' Then we realised there was a funny smell. And we went over. And where he'd flung the bag of E, they'd melted on top of a light bulb. So it was really bad.

PH: WHAT DID YOU SAY TO YOUR DAD?

SM: Nothing. He never said anything. It wasn't until my sister had said to him, 'Look, Alan and Susan are getting up to all sorts of things between them, all sorts of substances are being taken.' And I think he was just paranoid it was heroin. He says to me, 'Listen, I hope you're not dabbling in any of that'. I said 'No dad.' He was like, 'Is it?' I just kind of walked away going, 'Fuck!' I kind of upset him.

PH: WERE YOU IN L.A. WITH ALAN WHEN HE HAD HIS BREAKDOWN?

SM: Well previous to that I'd been in Rotherhithe where he'd been taking pure MDMA. It was Christmas or New Year. He freaked out then and had a minor freak out. And then the night before we went to L.A. to watch Primal Scream rehearsing. We were doing a week in L.A. then

ALAN McGEE AND THE STORY OF CREATION RECORDS

a week in New York. I'm meeting up with Primal Scream because they were doing an MTV Special with George Clinton. So the night before we went away Bob watched them and we got drunk and then they all came back to Rotherhithe. And we were all just getting madder at the night. And then we all went to the airport completely mad with it. I mean, I don't even remember!

I mean I remember Alan saying, 'Any questions they ask you just say yes to them all.' I was just standing there going, 'Yes. Yes.' Then Alan gave me a valium so I would sleep on the plane. And we fell asleep. Woke up about four hours later and Alan's sitting up the back of the plane surrounded by all these air hostesses. And I was going, 'No way. What's he doing? He's trying to pull already!' So I went up there and he's saying 'I'm having a *mad* time.' So I had to sit with him the whole time on the plane and say to him like, 'It's okay' and 'You're gonna be alright. Calm down. Don't worry,' and stuff to keep him together. But I was still completely freaking out. He thought he was alright and we went out that night. We went to the Whisky-a-Gogo.

PH: JACK DANIELS. WAS THAT WITH JESUS AND MARY CHAIN?

SM: No. They weren't with him. I think he was going to see them doing a video. Maybe they were with him, I can't remember. I met up with my pal who was living out there at the time. And we passed Keanu Reeves. And I was saying, 'No way.' I went to see Universal Studios and do all those kinds of things. And I came back into the hotel and they said, 'Listen.'

I came back and there was a phone call.

PH: Cedars Sinai?

SM: Cedars Sinai. He'd obviously phoned 911 as he freaked out in his hotel room. I went in and he was all tubed up on this stretcher. But at the same time, he was still on the mobile phone. So, while they were stretchering him away to the hospital, he was asking the receptionist out! Getting wheeled out on the stretcher and still have the balls to ask someone out. This is what he was like at this time like: a real womaniser.

PH: WHO WAS HE ON THE MOBILE PHONE TO?

SM: I don't know. Being Alan, phoning everyone going, 'I've just had a nervous breakdown.' Or 'Guess what's happened to me?' Or maybe he was just phoning a girl that he had asked out, I don't know. But he kind of, he had all these girls in America helping him back to health for the next two weeks as well.

ALAN McGEE

ALAN McGEE: You get a few warning shots across your bows. I had six. The one that I should have responded to was that Christmas when I got some sort of MDMA and me, Grant Fleming, Simone and Alex Nightingale took this particular batch of pure MDMA. Not all together. Me and Nightingale took it with Grant Fleming and his missus at the time, Jenny Mitchell. And we all had breakdowns or semi-breakdowns. I mean Simone had a breakdown because of it. I had a breakdown because of it. Grant lived in a storage cupboard above Alex Nightingale's office for about a year. I'd call that a breakdown! I don't know what he wants to call it. It was pretty bizarre. He was very bizarre for a long time right. The only person that came out of that unscarred is Alex-fucking-Nightingale. I don't know what he's made of – but it's definitely not blood and fucking tissue right? Anyway, I had an event in my house and I did about maybe a gram of pure MDMA. I don't know how many E that's the equivalent of but I think it's potentially maybe about 35 or something. I think I nearly overdosed that Christmas. I was in the house and I definitely had psychosis. I definitely went somewhere else for about three hours. They talked me back into reality. And when I say I'd been over the edge, that I looked over the edge of insanity and pulled myself back across back into reality, it would be an extreme understatement.

PAOLO McGEE: WAS THAT HOW IT FELT?
AM: That was the one time . . . If ever I was gonna go it was that day. I looked in the mirror and honestly, I really did think I was gonna go. Any

sane person would have pulled out at that point and went, 'That is it!' But I was so off my nut I kept fucking going. I had about ten days in my bed after that experience. I had Christmas in my bed absolutely ill. And then I started on the drugs again mid-January. I had a lot of serious sessions. Went down to see Primal Scream and it was just all fucking models and, sure enough, half of them ended back at my gaff with Abbot with a big load of cocaine. And this is how out of synch with fucking real life we were, me and Abbot. We put on Led Zeppelin and we've got two bi-sexual models lying in the couch getting into each other right. They were trying to provoke me and Abbot into some sort of heterosexual response right. And all me and Abbot did basically was dance with each other, punching the air and going, 'Rock 'n' roll'. And we've got two women just lying on the couch, touching each other's breasts, getting off with each other. Any sane person would have crawled in between them. And of course 7 a.m. and me and Abbot look at each other and go, 'Where did the lesbians go?'

PH: They'd gone?

AM: Yeah. Fed up. They went home and we never did anything about it. Then I got the kind of flu bug and I should have not been going out because Susan was coming, and I went down to see the Primals on the Friday night. We were flying out on the Sunday and hung with them when they were rehearsing.

PH: WHEREABOUTS WAS THAT? IN LONDON?

AM: I'll tell you where they were. Waterloo. The rehearsal studio. I can't remember what it's called. And I went down there and hung with the boys and it was good and everything like that. And then the next day Susan arrived and I went, 'I tell you what. We'll go down, take you down to see the Primals rehearse.' And I had the flu. And when you've got the flu the last thing you would want to do is lines of charlie with Throb. He racks them out for everybody. This was Throb at the height of cocaine mania. And he racks one out and suddenly we're into a night of madness right. And then everybody's back at mine and we're up till 10 a.m. I just remember before flying off to America I'd been in *NME* that week or the week before and Throb going, 'Oh McGee, double respect.' For the quote 'Your girlfriend can come and go but the Rolling Stones last forever!' 'Double respect McGee.' So me and Susan get on the plane. I'm fine and then suddenly it's as if I am on an acid trip. I thought I was gonna die. I thought I was having a heart attack.

PH: You're still in London?

AM: No no. I'm now two hours into a flight to Los Angeles. I've got another nine hours to go. I've got no downers. I've got no valium. I've got no fucking tranquilizers. I've got no Tamazepan. The stewardess thought I was on acid. I wasn't on acid. I'd only been doing coke the whole night. But you know, the fucking MDMA experience about seven or eight weeks before had unfurled the fucking flag. It started to unravell during the flight due to the fact that I'd had no sleep and loads and loads of drugs. It's coming unfurled. And it was actually quite comical some of it. The stewardess is coming up to me and saying, 'Are you on acid?' And I was going, 'No I'm not on fucking acid!' I couldn't tell them I'd been caning drugs all night.

I was met off the plane by paramedics and they just said, 'You've got nervous exhaustion.' It's a nice way of saying: you've got to stop taking drugs and go to rehab. And I said, 'I'll be alright'. I got back, went straight to bed and then got up about 4 p.m. and I was very tired, but because I was with Susan I kind of felt as if I had to show her a good time. She was my little sister and I had to look after her and family stuff like that. We went to see Swervedriver. Any sane person would at this point say, 'Enough. You nearly died at Christmas and you've just had a nervous breakdown on the fucking plane. Go home you daft cunt and fucking get better.'

So I went out and did about a bottle of Jack Daniels. It was never the same again. I lost the plot. The next day I got up and Susan said, 'You must stop taking drugs. You must.' Susan is nine years younger than me and she's pleading with me to stop taking drugs! I went into the other room and fucking downed loads of diet pills and mad shit like that. I was just a total addict.

I went to lunch with somebody and started feeling fucking strange, but I still haven't got my head around how strange it is. I went on to have a meeting with Lenny Waronker about Primal Scream and some movie soundtrack. And as I was driving there I was getting really tense. My toes were fucking curling up and I was getting fucking cramps in my stomach and starting to feel really freaky, but I was keeping it together. I got into the building and I'm walking through still not feeling on top of it, but riding it like a bad drug trip. And I'm walking through and the blinds start moving towards me, blinds were like moving in my vision. And at that point, I said, 'I'm going mad. Fuck I am actually going mad.' I had to immediately turn out of the building, get in the car and I had to drive over the hill and in the middle of all this I got this thing, which now I know is called hypertension. Your bones go so stiff and it feels as if somebody had put a steel rod into you. I don't ever want to feel that ever again.

So, anyway, I go back to the hotel and I took all my clothes off, went under the shower to try and calm down. Lying on my bed naked and trying to fucking chill with it. At that precise point I thought, 'Fuck's sake.' So I phoned down, panicking, and said, 'Man, I think I'm gonna die. My heart's gonna go.' Basically, what I'm doing is uncorking seven years of total fucking abuse. Because this is nay like the speed pills I've taken that morning: this is the beginning of the end, if you know what I mean. I said, 'You'd better get me a doctor.' And sure enough the fucking paramedics arrive.

I met them downstairs in the lobby and I did want to come clean but I didn't want to tell them I'd been taking loads of drugs. So I went, 'I was drinking a lot and took some speed pills today.' So the paramedics sit me in a fucking wheelchair and they take my pulse and my blood pressure is way over 170. Paolo, your blood pressure is supposed to between 103 and 108. At that point they said, 'We're taking you to hospital. We're scared that you have a blood clot, Mr McGee. We've got to do this. Put that on.' So then take me into this big fuck-off wagon and lie me down and won't let me move. And at this point I think 'I'm in a bad movie; I'm in a shitey B-movie version.'

Susan had been off for the day to the L.A. Zoo and so she got herself back to the hotel and phoned, 'Where are you?' And I went, 'I'm in the hospital. I've got IV drips in me.' She started crying. She came round, and she said, 'My God, what am I gonna do with you? Dad's gonna go mental.' And I said, 'I don't want you to tell my dad, you fucking idiot.' She was really good with me. I've said, 'I'm a drug addict.' And she said, 'If you ever take drugs again I'm gonna punch you in the mouth.'

That was the turning point. There's a point were everybody cleans up. And that was it for me. They were putting oxygen on me, I thought I was gonna have a blood clot and that was the point that I went, 'Alright. I've done my bit for rock 'n' roll. It's over. No more.'

PH: HOW DID YOUR DAD RESPOND? YOU BOTH WERE SCARED OF TELLING HIM ABOUT THIS NEAR DEATH EXPERIENCE.

AM: It would have been hard for my dad to tell me off. Rock 'n' roll had retired my dad at the age of 61. I had given him £100,000 when I did the deal with Sony. I went, 'There you go old guy. Fucking chuck your crappy fucking rat-race job where you compete with 35-year-old men for fucking estimates and car sales.' I mean, I hope you and me aren't in the rat race at 61 trying to compete with fucking 35-year-olds. So it would be almost hypocritical for him to tell me to stop it.

PH: So he knew about it?

AM: He knew about it. But to be fair I always said, 'I've got it under control. I'm just dabbling.' Susan knew how deep I was in but my dad never knew how deep I was in.

PH: Is this when you call Ed?

AM: I got a call from Noel. In the midst of this, he'd heard that I'd got ill. Sony had heard I was ill. I'd holed up there not taking calls for 12 days right. Meanwhile, Dick and Abbot were at a kind of war with each other around this time.

PH: They were arguing while this was going on?

AM: They were jockeying for position. Dick was my right-hand man. Abbot was trying to become my right-hand man. So there was a bit of jockeying for it right. They were putting calls in and kind of complaining about each other.

I had fucking completely lost the plot so I could only take about fucking 20 minutes of phone calls a day and then I'd put the phone off the hook.

PH: DID THEY KNOW THAT YOU HAD HAD THIS BREAKDOWN?
AM: I'd had a lot of fucking drug experiences where I'd been out of action days. I'd had the Christmas episode of 10 or 12 days in my bed. Abbot always said to me, 'I've never known anybody that had a position of fucking respectability – if you can call running a record company a position of respectability – that did as many street drugs as you McGee'. I mean, I'd rolled out of so many scrapes with drugs, there were times that I should never have really kind of come back.

PH: SO YOU HOLE UP IN THE HOTEL?
AM: Yep and I got a call through from Noel. But in the meantime some girl who was like a big, big Creation fan had found out that I was in town and she came up with cakes for me.
PH: Hash cakes?
AM: No, not hash cakes. Cake cakes. She came up. I wasn't having sex with her. I think she was a virgin. So Susan phones my gran and I get put on the phone and I'm absolutely off my nut. My gran says 'Oh, what are you up to son?' I said, 'I've met this girl, a new girlfriend. She's a virgin'. And my gran replied 'Yeah, vergin' on ridiculous.'

Then this girl ran me down to see the Mary Chain who were in town. And the Mary Chain immediately go, 'Are you on any medication?' And I went, 'Yeah, I'm on these valium.' They said 'Can you give us some?' And I went, 'Alright'.
PH: So you still weren't taking it seriously.
AM: I was thinking: 'I'm Alan McGee. I'm indestructible. I'm gonna bounce through this fucking thing.'

PH: DID YOU DO AN *NME* INTERVIEW AROUND THIS TIME?
AM: No I did that the month before in L.A. with Keith Cameron.
PH: Because Jeff Barrett said an interesting thing. He said, 'I read that

interview and I just thought he's gone mate, he's off his tits. McGee, the King of Indie is being interviewed by a pool in Los Angeles . . . '

AM: See now, if you'd said that three years ago I would have probably got defensive about that comment. But you know something, Barrett's right, I had lost the plot. I had absolutely lost the plot.

INTERLUDE

TIM & CHRIS ABBOT

I went to Bethnal Green and met up with Tim and Chris Abbot. The interview that followed was revealing, hilarious, scandalous and totally incomprehensible. I think the main thing they wanted to get across was not to respond to criticisms of them from people within Creation – 'they were fucking water carriers, we were the menaces' – but to highlight the Infinite label that Chris ran. This was mainly Detroit House, which added a dimension to Creation which has gone unnoticed.

The following excerpt is the only part from the interview – which, admittedly, took place with cans and the goodness on board – that I could salvage and present to you, the reader.

TIM ABBOT: Having fucking dropped out, I'd say between '86 and '88, I went to Thailand with 50 E came back within six months, fucking lost my licence, lost the company, and lost my fucking house. And it was like 'These pills are great, they really do work' There's a great story right when Steve Mason at the time was the richest, the biggest-salaried man in the music business.

CHRIS ABBOT: Yeah. They had a massive meeting to renegotiate the distribution or something. The biggest meeting of the year. So I'd been away and got this builder in. It was about lunchtime. These people are coming in the meeting at about 2.30 p.m. and there's about 15 minutes to go. This old guy just walks in and I'm . . .

TA: Mega story. This is a great story.

CA: . . . trying to get the attention of Anita on the desk and she . . .

TA: She was on the phone.

CA: . . . was on the phone and this bloke comes in – just walks straight in and goes down towards the bunker. So I turned around and said, 'Excuse me. Where do you think you're going.' The bloke replied, 'I'm going for a shit.' I said, 'You what?' He says, 'I'm going for a shit!'

I said, 'You fucking what? What do you think you're fucking doing walking off the street and coming down?' And he's absolutely wrecked; he's been in the pub all lunchtime.

TA: Screaming paddy.

CA: Tim said, 'Excuse me, who are you?'

TA: 'Who the fuck are you?'

CA: It all goes off. Next thing you know, the bloke comes up and head-butts me. Fucking hell, big fight kicks off in the reception.

TA: A wild diabetic and a pissed paddy rolling around just before the big meeting. Unbelievable.

CA: Next thing, the bell goes, just as the fight explodes in the living room. The paddy is going absolutely bonkers.

TA: I've got him in a lock haven't I. And Anita's saying, 'He's going purple.' And I'm saying, 'If I let go of him he will go purple – and kill us all.' He was mad wasn't he?

CA: Next thing you know door's buzzed open, Steve Mason and all the people.

TA: Suited up.

CA: 'Hello,' 'Hello,' 'Aah'.

TA: And I've said, 'It won't affect the meeting. Would you go downstairs.'

CA: 'Shall we come back in about ten minutes?'

TA: 'No,' I said, 'No.' We sent them downstairs didn't we. 'Anita, call the fucking police before I choke him.'

CA: Pet. When the police came.

TA: The girls didn't like actually me having Anita in there. She was great. She would come in with a fucking seven-inch micro skirt, bare fucking legs and loads of shit in her hair. The company was out of control. It was fantastic.

CHAPTER SIX

SIMON STEPHENS: You've got to remember there's like 20 people on this Scream tour. 18 did drugs. That's all the crew and all the band, everybody involved apart from Denise (vocals) and Henry (bass) who didn't do anything. So we're all fucking at it and all of a sudden it all welled up. I used to be knocking on Throb's door going, 'Give me some gear.' I forgot I had a job to do, and it all just went to pot. Once the brown came in that was it. Thankfully, Innes and Bob sat down and said 'This can't go on, we're supposed to be making music, look at these fucking idiots around us.' To be fair, Bobby would have a little lick now and again. Innes would just fucking do it because he knew he could handle it. And he could handle it. I always said, either people die or get out of it forever. I'll never ever do it again.

ED BALL: If you take Alan out of the equation, it all falls to bits. It's like that game Ker-plunk. You take Alan out of it and everything crumbles because everyone's relationship is to do with Alan. Everyone comes on board because they want to deal with the captain. It's like Captain Bligh in *Mutiny on the Bounty*.

SS: I could see the signs there. We did two tours in America. Alan turned up on the second one and we were at it. We had people in L.A. that used to come and meet us. We're from a council estate in Brighton and they used to come and meet us. I've got a vivid memory of Alan turning up in L.A. and all the big honchos were there from Sire records and Warners. I just remember looking at him and thinking, 'Yeah, I feel the same as you. I'm not as rich as you, I'm not as famous as you and I haven't got as much as you, but I also feel really fucking empty about all this. There's somewhere in the middle that's so fucking empty.' Alan was in a fucking jidder-juddery paranoid state.

EB: I was in Tokyo with the Boo Radleys and Kle phoned me up and said, 'Ed, can you go to L.A. and pick up Alan, he's blown up.

He's in the hotel room and he won't leave. He's asked for you to come and get him. Says either you or his Dad.' So I went off from there back to London and then got another plane although I'm sure it would have been quicker the other way. When I got there, he was in the Hyatt, a really tall hotel and I have never seen him so white. He was really white and quite sort of fragile. Perhaps this was the only time I've ever seen him and then just hugged him. He really did look shot to pieces.

KLE: I've had some anxiety problems and I get panic attacks and it helped me out at Creation when Alan had his breakdown because I was sympathetic to him. I could understand. They didn't understand what was happening to him. It was, 'You're not ill, you're not throwing up, so what's wrong with you?'

They didn't understand it and a lot of them were just a little bit too off their head and still having a good time to really get it through their heads. When Alan started to feel really bad, he started to seclude himself, for obvious reasons, because people were always ringing him up just to talk about any little problem, especially if they were having that problem with Dick or anybody else. It would always be Alan that they'd want to ring as if he had some magic wand. In a way he did. He could override anybody's decision but it was a lot of pressure to put on this person who is just trying to make records and when he did have the breakdown there was a very small inner sanctum of people who did see him every day. That's when our relationship switched from being more of a professional boss and his assistant to a bond of *real* friendship.

LAURENCE: I lost faith in him and talked to the wrong people. I didn't want to have anything to do with Alan to the point when Alan had that bad thing in America. I had people phoning me up and asking me to confirm it and I said, 'Piss off I'm not talking.' Alan and I became friends again – I met him in the street when he was still very unstable and not mixing with people.

K: It was really just myself, Ed, and Alan's father – who'd come down a lot during Alan's recovery, especially when he was put on the course of valium. We'd sit around and talk about books and movies and relationships and people and things like that. It was a special time for us. It was a hard time for him but when he emerged out of it he was a way stronger person, more focused and with a different lease of life. There are a few people that weren't there for him and he was quite hurt. I don't think anyone abandoned him on purpose. I think people weren't calling because they were too scared. It took him a long time to forgive and forget it. But at the end of the day Alan's the kind of person that does understand where somebody else is coming from. He doesn't think the world revolves around him and his outlook.

MARK GARDNER: I was really scared because he had said to me as well that I had a bit of a side to me which could potentially be quite damaging as well and I should keep it in check. This was one of the first conversations I had with him soon after he'd broken down.

JEFF BARRETT: It became two separate things. Alan McGee and Creation. I think the soul of it really had gone.

L: Johnny Hopkins was given Oasis because he could relate to them musically. I didn't give a shit about Oasis. I knew they would do well – not that well – but what kind of a life is it? Johnny would argue over his mobile phone for an hour during dinner parties with *Sun* journalists who were about to run a story. What kind of a life is that?

SUSAN McGEE: Alan has got such a strength of character. Every week he would set himself personal goals. There was still loads of drive there. It was a kind of weird time. He was pretty nervous you know. So I suppose that was pretty much a confidence thing. But then if you shut yourself away and you don't speak to anyone then your confidence does go because you've got nothing to say to anyone.

He got himself together again basically. And then he saw Doctor Brewer, who was a great help to him. One night, Bobby phoned him and said 'Kurt Cobain's just died.' The Primals were playing that night and Alan said, you've got to dedicate a song to him. And I went to the gig and Bobby being Bobby was so out of his face he didn't pronounce it properly. He just kind of said, 'Kurt Cobain died' and everyone cheered because they thought he'd said 'Primal Scream'.

EB: He'd be alright, as long he didn't put himself in some of the same situations. He drives himself. That's always been the thing with Alan. He finds an obsession and then drives himself relentlessly to fulfil it and to be the best at it. It's not competitive as in, 'I'm the best, you're a bunch of cunts. I'm still standing and you're all dead.' No it's that he just drives himself on and on and on. So as long as he wasn't going to do that I thought he was going to be alright.

ALAN McGEE

ALAN McGEE: Noel was great around that time. He'd come up to Rotherhithe to take me for dinner. He was one of the few really honest people around me. He was great. So was Andy Bell. Him and his wife used to come and stay the night with me and my dad when we were holed up in the fucking penthouse in Rotherhithe. I remember saying, 'I've lost my ego.' And he went, 'John Lennon said that when he had done too much acid.' I had went, 'Fine Andy but I'm never gonna get it back.' I got my ego back in about '97. I think it's quite a powerful thing because it makes you do things. I think that the casualties in the friendships were the Primals really. What happened was that they were the ones that were doing the drugs with me more than anybody else. The only thing that was really gluing it all together was the drugs. I mean Bobby came around and we'd basically sit and watch a video of him on stage playing some place like Southampton with two thousand people. We'd sit and watch his video and he'd go, 'Have you got any medication?' I'd say 'I've got this big tub of valium.' He'd do like 40 valium or something mental. I'd be on valium because I was losing my mind and he would be on valium because he was *trying* to lose his mind. It was weird. Really, really weird. We were drifting. And then he went off on that American tour and to be fair it was a black hole of Calcutta that they were getting involved in.

PAOLO HEWITT: Supporting Depeche Mode?

AM: Yeah. 16 week American tour. This was really the breaking point. We only patched it up in the last year. But he never phoned me for months. He came back off that tour and I was utterly pissed with him because my self-esteem by this point was miserable. I thought the only people who want to know me are people that think I can do something for them. The Primals never phoned for four months. In retrospect, I now think I was like looking at a mirror for them – it could have been any one of them. On that tour they were losing their minds and when they got back it was like, 'We want to see Alan.' By that point, me being me, I just went, 'Fuck off, I don't want to know you man.' We never really spoke again until about November of that year when I came back down to London. It was really difficult for me to come back to London.

PH: WHEREABOUTS HAD YOU GONE?

AM: First of all I was in London until about June. I was in Rotherhithe in this big fucking penthouse. My dad went home at the beginning of June because he was getting married in September that year. My dad lived with me for about three months.

PH: AND WHAT DID YOU DO DURING THE DAYS?

AM: Nothing. I was just going in and out of panic attacks. I was seeing a psychiatrist every week and I was on medication. The guy was going, 'Look, we don't need to put him in a fucking hospital. You're all there Mr McGee.' The doctor was on call for me. I could phone him up on his mobile and all that bollocks. So we got through that period. My dad went back and then I had a mini-breakdown. I was walking around this man-made lake in Rotherhithe and I knew I had lost the plot because I had been round it about eight times. I phoned up Ed Ball and I went, 'Man, you've got to come and get me.' And he replies, 'Meet me half-way because it will take me about two hours to get from mine to yours. Meet me in an hour in Camden.' I got in the taxi and went up. I saw Ed. He was the only person I could really phone.

That's why I fucking adore him so much because he never shirked. He always was there for us. He went, 'Fuck man, I think you are really ill.' And I went, 'I'm really fucking depressed.' And he went, 'Right, you're gonna have to go home Alan to your dad. I'll move into the flat and make sure you're alright but I think you should go home.' I phoned my dad and then Ed came back with me and stayed for about another day and then my dad flew down and took me home to Scotland. My dad's new girlfriend's – who then became his wife, who's amazing – daughter moved out of the house so that I could move in. It was amazing. I started to remember when I moved to Scotland. I was caught up in this London set of people, coming round on Sunday afternoon watching the football, with me getting out fucking four grams and throwing it on the table and caning it while watching some Wimbledon versus West Ham game thinking it was a good game and doing as much of it as possible, then going, 'Is Weatherall playing?' We'd go off to do some more. But sitting round people in Scotland, not buying into any of the fucking bullshit whatsoever I started getting myself back together. And then the doctor said, 'You're stable with the drugs, we can bring you down to London'. And then I went into six weeks of therapy.

PH: IS THIS IN THE REHAB PLACE IN LISSON GROVE?
AM: Lisson Grove. They had me in there for six weeks and it was two doctors every day going through my childhood and all this shit came out about what my problem with life was.

PH: DID THEY GO BACK TO THE PROBLEMS WITH YOUR MUM AND DAD?
AM: It was all that. That was really the core of what was bugging me out and we got to the bottom of all that and then I went back home to Scotland. And I was chucking the music business. Oasis were number One with *Definitely Maybe* but I was chucking it. I was arsed. I mean my attitude to all of it was, 'I'll buy a Barratt house for £100,000, I've got two million in the bank, I'll live off the interest. Susan was introducing me to girls and shit like that but I wasn't interested any more. I became asexual for about a year. I suppose it was because I was on medication, it probably fucks your sex drive. But the other side of the coin is I just had no self-confidence. But after sitting up there for two weeks I just thought, 'Man, don't give in. Don't fucking give in.' It was nothing to do with, 'Go back you deserve your acclaim because Oasis are now the biggest group in the world.' It wasn't anything like that. Do you know

what it was? It was, 'McGee, you're made of strong shit. Don't just give in man, go back and make yourself better. The only place you can do it is London. Glasgow is lovely but it's not your home. London's your home. That's where you've made your life.' So I came back down and I saw Bobby and it was really double fucking awkward. We made a peace, that he probably thought was a peace but it was never a peace in my head. A peace was made but in my head there was a massive grudge going on there.

PH: YOU STILL FELT BETRAYED BY THEM?
AM: Utterly betrayed and, in retrospect, wrongly because they had their own set of problems.

PH: WAS THAT THEIR POINT OF VIEW?
AM: Yeah. And I think it was probably true.

PH: DID THEY FEEL THAT YOU DIDN'T HELP THEM WHEN THEY NEEDED IT?
AM: No because they knew that I was incapable of helping anybody.

SUSAN McGEE

SUSAN McGEE: He fancied her. He watched the Frasier Chorus video that was on and he was sitting with Belinda and he was saying, 'She's really good looking.' Then he met her a couple of years down the line through Laurence. You know Laurence?

PAOLO HEWITT: I interviewed her for the book.

SM: She's amazing isn't she. And Laurence got the two of them hitched up. But Alan was still not well when he started going out with Kate. I think he had been through a lot of girlfriends who were just after him for what he was, but Kate came from a different background. It wasn't like she was after him for money because she's pretty middle class – but not snotty. She's pretty right-on. She was really such a strong character for him and she practically bosses him about, which is brilliant because he needs that.

KATE HOLMES

PAOLO HEWITT: HOW DID YOU MEET ALAN?

KATE HOLMES: I met him through a friend, Laurence.

PH: How did you know Laurence?

KH: I'd known her for years just from the Indie scene really. And then, I was house-sitting a flat in Belsize Park and she said, 'Oh, Alan's come out of hospital and he wants to take people out to dinner because he needs company really, not sexual company just interesting people. He's always expressed an interest in you. Would you go out for dinner with him?' I went, 'Yeah, fine.'

PH: WHAT DID YOU DO BEFORE THIS?

KH: I was in a band called Frasier Chorus. And then I worked for Youth for a bit and got my own deal. I've been doing music since I was about 17. I worked for the Mad Professor ever since I was a student.

PH: Mad Professor. He's a bit of a name, isn't he?

KH: Yeah. I Played on about 20 of his albums.

PH: Did you? What do you play?

KH: Flute.

PH: So you go out for dinner. You obviously knew him anyway.

KH: I actually met him at a Slowdive gig. Slowdive were having a party and I met him there. Just went to Blacks for a drink and he asked for my phone number. So I gave it to him. He phoned me after about two weeks. And I went out to dinner with him.

PH: You must have known about him anyway.

KH: Not really. I wasn't the Creation girl. I was into Cocteau Twins and

178

Pixies and I loved the whole 4AD sort of ethic. Frasier Chorus, first signing was at 4AD.

PH: HADN'T YOU READ ABOUT ALAN THOUGH IN THE PRESS?
KH: Yeah. Maybe in the press, but they didn't really make an impression to be honest. I wasn't a Creation groupie or anything. He was quite difficult to be with that year because he'd just come out of hospital.
PH: In one of the interviews I did with Alan, I said to him, 'How did people treat you when you came out?' And he said, 'Everybody was tip-toeing around me except for Kate and she got a lot of stick for it.'
KH: I was quite hard on him. I wasn't in awe of him. If he did something that was out of order, I'd just say to him straight away. He didn't like it. And everybody else was saying, 'Yes Alan. Three bags full, Alan.' He was surrounded by sycophants. And I was going around saying, 'No, Alan.' And I thought he didn't like it and he used to tell me to get lost. 'Well okay then, I'm going.' And I'd just disappear for a couple of weeks. That was my tactic. And soon after about a week you know . . .
PH: Phone would start ringing?
KH: He'd start ringing me up. It happened about 15 times that first year.

PH: WHAT SORT OF THINGS WAS IT? WHAT SORT OF THINGS WOULD HE HAVE DONE? CAN YOU JUST GIVE ME ONE EXAMPLE?
KH: I really can't remember, Paolo, sorry. All that is sort of in the past.
PH: Would it have been things he said?
KH: Yeah, things like that. Or I'd go, 'That's not right.' And then he'd go, 'But it is.' And it was that sort of thing. I really can't remember specifics.
PH: And were people at work tip-toeing around him?
KH: Yes, they were. He was fragile.

PH: WHEN YOU SAY 'FRAGILE' DO YOU MEAN IN A PHYSICAL, OR A MENTAL WAY?
KH: Not physically fragile, mentally fragile. But you would be after a breakdown wouldn't you?

PH: You would.

KH: I think he recovered really quickly. He got his full strength back within about a year.

PH: He told me two and a half.

KH: Oh did he? Two and a half it is then. Being generous. He was scared to go on planes and things. I made him travel. I booked holidays and said, 'I'm going, with or without you.' And he'd just go, 'Alright. I'll come then.' So it kind of got him stronger. He had to face up to going abroad.

PH: And what about going to gigs?

KH: I wouldn't. I'm not a great gig person anyway. We still went to gigs together. We went to see Oasis and stuff. And I was the one that drank a bottle of champagne and was absolutely legless.

PH: You drank in front of him? You didn't feel like awkward?

KH: Yeah. I still drink in front of him. I mean he can still drink if he wants, it's just a personal thing that he doesn't drink. It's not like he's not allowed ever to drink again. If he wants to have a drink, he can, but he doesn't want to. So, you know, he's never asked me not to drink and I probably wouldn't. I'd just say, 'No.'

PH: WAS THERE A LOT OF PRESSURE ON HIM WHEN HE WENT BACK TO WORK? I MEAN THE OASIS THING HAD TAKEN OFF AND IT WAS ALL MENTAL.

KH: I don't think so. I think he quite enjoyed it.

PH: HOW WAS HIS RELATIONSHIP WITH OASIS AT THAT TIME? HAD IT KIND OF CALMED DOWN?

KH: A little bit, yeah. I mean he still spoke to the boys on the phone. I think as they got bigger and bigger, they had more of a a corporate management strategy. I think that if a band gets that big, the management becomes more powerful.

PH: And what about the Primals? Because he was quite upset with their perceived lack of support throughout his illness.

KH: I think he was. I think, that's one thing that I can claim: I got him back with Bobby.

PH: How did you do that?

KH: Alan was angry for quite a few years and I just would explain that people just can't always help it. Sometimes they just run away from fear. If someone's ill they just can't cope because they're ill themselves. I had a four hour conversation with Bobby while Alan was away. He came back to the house and everything. Bobby was sort of telling me how much he loved Alan. I was going, 'He loves you too, but you've just got to sort it out. It's ridiculous.' After that they started talking again.

PH: Was this when he was in New York and Alan was in London?

KH: Yeah. They had a big row .

PH: Ed Ball's another close friend isn't he?

KH: Yeah. I'm not close to Ed but I think it's because he's got that friendship with him. I really like Ed but he's like Alan's sort of main friend.

PH: DO YOU THINK ALAN MAKES FRIENDS EASILY?

KH: He makes women friends really easily. Male friends not so easily.

PH: Well as far as I can see it's Ed and Bobby really.

KH: Yeah. It's women he gets on better with.

PH: Why is that?

KH: I think he's a very sensitive person. He likes women. He's not chauvinistic at all. They sort of love him.

PH: SO WHO ARE HIS WOMEN FRIENDS AT THE MOMENT? KLE?

KH: Kle, yeah. Gemma he's really close to as well. His sister Susan as well.

PH: What about Laura?

KH: He's getting closer to her now.

PH: He is? Because there was a big competition thing when they were growing up wasn't there?

KH: But they're talking now and are getting on better than ever.

PH: I remember watching that *Omnibus* documentary they did on Alan, and I remember thinking, 'Why are you in music?' He just talked about football for the whole programme.

KH: That's quite funny because he was obsessed with football for years but now he's gone off football.

PH: Gone back into music?

KH Yeah, which is quite telling really.

PH: Would you call him an obsessive character?

KH: Completely.

PH: DOES THAT OBSESSION EVER GET IN THE WAY OF YOUR RELATIONSHIP?

KH: It used when he phoned me up 15 times a day. I used to turn the phone off.

PH: That's quite a lot isn't it? Were you trying to save his phone bill?

KH: No, I was trying to save my ear. He's stopped that now. He doesn't phone me for two days when he's away and I get really worried. The first day I met him, I was at his flat and he opened the door and offered me a drink. He had a shelf on the fridge that was filled from the bottom to the top with Purdeys. And that lasted about a month. And after that it was grapes. He'd eat 20 pounds of grapes a day. And then it was oranges. And it was muesli. Then it was rice cakes. Now its cornflakes and coffee.

PH: DO YOU THINK MONEY HAS CHANGED HIM?

KH: It made him a bit more cocky. Money just gives you a kind of freedom.

PH: The last time I met him was in here and he'd just been to some meeting. I wanted to talk to him about stuff, but he was kind of a bit distracted. He finally says, 'Paolo I'm really sorry. I've just come from a meeting where I've been told by a load of lawyers that if I do this and do that and if I move this here and if I move that there, Poptones will be worth £30 million. I said 'That's good.' And he replied, 'Yeah, but I'm just a chancer. My buzz is the game, not the winning. Its the actual game.'

KH: We don't have a particularly affluent lifestyle.

PH: He told me that you've had to step in a few times and say, 'That's far too much.' When he's tried to donate money to something.

KH: He gives a lot of it away.

PH: Who does he give it to?

KH: He'll give some to charity. I had to stop him giving another £50,000 to the Labour Party last year.

PH: DO YOU SHARE HIS PASSION FOR MUSIC?
KH: No.
PH: You don't? You don't like buying albums, etc?
KH: I love music. We like different sorts of things really. I like ethereal music and he likes all the old stuff.
PH: Sex Pistols?
KH: Yeah. I can't stand the Sex Pistols.
PH: You can't stand them? You can't stand rock music?
KH: Not really, no.
PH: Too loud, noisy and . . .
KH: Too masculine for me. I did love the Mary Chain. The first album, I bought when I was a student. I love music but I'm not as passionate about it as he is.
PH: Do you ever worry that he'll ever go back on the drugs or anything?
KH: No. He never will.
PH: He won't? That's it?
KH: He's got too much self-will. He had such a massive panic attack on the plane that its etched in his memory, and he won't want to put himself through that. He's health conscious and wouldn't want to destroy his body like that again.
PH: There is a bit in my interview with him where he's saying that he's in the back of the cab going back to the hotel and he was just falling to pieces. He said that he suddenly felt as though there was a steel rod been put into him. He said that he never wanted to feel like that again.
KH: He'll never go back on. He might have a drink one year when he's about 50 or something. But I mean he's such an addictive personality that if he had one drink he will probably want the whole bottle. I'm not addictive at all. I'm the complete opposite. I can say no to anything.
PH: So does this balance it out?
KH: Yeah. And like he's hedonistic and I'm not. He's obsessive and I'm not. And that's quite a good balance. He's fun to be with. He makes me

laugh all the time. That's the main thing. I think that's what women really want from men in the long run is someone who can make them laugh, make them feel good about themselves and adore them. And that's what I get from Alan.

ALAN McGEE

ALAN McGEE: It's a belief I had for five years, that they had betrayed me. And to be honest I probably never did any work on Primal Scream for the next five years. I never deliberately fucked them up, but I never deliberately tried to help them, do you know what I mean? And then that came to a head in '99 when me and Gillespie had two almighty humongous arguments – arguments to end all arguments. I had just got married and Paul Gallagher [spoof bridesmaid at McGee's wedding and Noel and Liam's brother] said that Bob had said or Innes had said something along the lines of, 'It's fashionable to get married.' As if I'd get married out of fucking trying to be fashionable. I'm not part of the *Hello* scenario. I don't even go out to parties. I don't even like parties because there's no point to me going to parties. I can't drink, can't take drugs, and I'm married. It's like parties to me are if I've got to go, I go, but there's no upside for me going to a party. So me getting married for the sake of trying to be fashionable, I found very offensive.

So that was the start of me and Gillespie and it was when he was in New York that we had a very, very, very bad argument and *all* the shit came out. And it was all like 'You weren't fucking there for me,' and him going, 'Well, you know, you are not the only person that's been ill.' And it was quite a base argument. And it was a really bad argument because he was still taking loads of gear and it never properly really went away.

PAOLO HEWITT: This all took place on the phone?

AM: It was a good 50-minute rant at each other. I've always been able to give Gillespie as good as he's ever going to get off anybody. So the arguments that we've had over a period of 25 years are still ugly but these two were the worst that we've ever had. That second one was the worst one. It was an abominable argument. Everything came out. Every bit of spleen. Me not trying to hurt him; and him not trying to hurt me. But all the fucking things that the Primals felt about me . . .

PH: WHAT DID THEY FEEL?
AM: They felt as if I didn't give a fuck about them. And you know, I didn't at that time. I couldn't have given a fuck whether they were on the label or whether they weren't on the label. And they knew that. But ultimately I did give a fuck about them. I wouldn't be having that argument with somebody if I didn't give a fuck. This had been building since '91. And '94 had been the breaking point because we had been living lifestyles and belief systems that were kind of growing apart. And then I got off the drugs and I was really low they weren't about for me. That was it. It was 'Fuck you then'. I knew that I wasn't well enough to have the argument. And if I'm ever going to have an argument with Bob I always make sure I'm fucking well enough to fucking have it with him.

So it was all that kind of going on. And during all this we had let a load of people go mid-way through '98. The people themselves didn't have a problem with getting let go. The only people that had a problem were Primal Scream. And again they had a word with Paul Gallagher about it. I don't think it was about Graham, Bob's brother, because I think he got a really good package. I think it was Joanne, Emily's sister. We'd let Emily's sister go and because Emily goes out with Bob, they thought that it was me being anti-them. Which it wasn't. I'm not going to have it with Emily's big sister, for fuck sake, I'm not a child.

So anyway I met Innes in the street and Innes bombs past. I went, 'Come here. What's all this shit?' Paul Gallagher is not the most discreet person in the world and Paul would come in and go, 'They wish they weren't on the label, they wish you'd drop them.' I just called them. I went to Innes, I went, 'If you want to go, go, get your lawyer and fuck off then. If you want to go, go.' Innes got really offended and got Bob and then they wanted to have a meeting with us. And then Bob, the dexadrine king, had obviously done like two dexy's before he came in. And the next hour right, it was like a blast furnace, un-fucking-believable argument right. Every bit of vitriol that me and him could hurt each other with was tossed at each other. But unbelievably, it fucking cleared the air. There is no point in telling you what we said to each other because it was a painful argument for me because things got said both sides that were beyond the pale. Next day I was hurting. He was gonna phone me that night but he never phoned. And then I phoned him at 10 a.m. and I said, 'We cannot have any more arguments like that because if we have any more arguments, we are just not going to be friends any more.' I was at the point of giving in completely with Bob. And he just said, 'As long as I can phone you about my business, let's just try and not fall out. I agree with you McGee. Because it's like we've got nothing in common with each other any more.' And it's ironic because we came to that decision and then we bonded again with each other. It's really weird right. And I said, 'Yeah, fair enough. I agree with you.' We were both utterly smarting from it.

And then I met him at Reading '98. I was trying to avoid him and he was trying to avoid me. And then about February '99 I got a phone call. He was flying near the edge and I think what happens when the chips are down you basically roll back to who your real mates are. And he fucking phoned me up and a proper peace was made between the two of us. I helped get his head back on track and ever since then, I must admit, it's kind of like the early '80s with me and Bob now. I mean it's fucking solid as a rock again. We're two best friends. And ever since then we've been close. I was involved with *Xtrmntr* whereas with *Shoulder of Giants*, I had absolutely nothing to do with it.

I had absolutely nothing to do with that album. The Primals were making *Xtrmntr*. And every week you'd get asked, 'What do you think of this?' This was the difference between the two big Creation bands. The Primals would ask me round the studio. You'd meet them in Primrose Hill and it would be, 'We've got this new track. It's called 'Blood Money', do you want to come and hear it?' Whereas you know with the last Oasis album that they did under us, it just felt as if we were the distribution company. And we had no part in it, no creative part in it.

AM: Probably the highest point for me was 'Supersonic' on *The Tube*, or whatever it was [*The Word*]. That is, when Liam had the camera and to me this was Oasis at their best. I was sitting there miserable as fuck in Scotland. But I did believe in this band, I just really believed in them. They fucking came on and you just knew that it was gonna go off man. But Knebworth was probably the greatest moment. That's the point where we won the war, it was like the end of World War II. 'Fucking hell, you are the fucking biggest group in the world at the moment.' Five skinny geezers. Working-class blokes from Manchester taking the fucking piss up on stage with 125,000 people watching. It's a merger: Punk rock and psychedelia. That's what it was.

I'd say my relationship with Noel was close up until about November '94. After that I think he always wanted my approval and he always wanted my respect which he will always have for the rest of his life, just because at the end of the day, he's a fucking genuinely loyal person and he's never let me down.

I'd say creatively, I was really involved in the first album. Marcus and Noel bringing mixes round to me, when I was still in Rotherhithe. I remember Noel coming round and playing mixes of the first album and he says, 'Have you got any Jack Daniels?' And I went, 'I think I might have somewhere.' I wasn't drinking any more. Susan was down looking after me. My dad had gone home. And I go and find this bottle of Jack Daniels. I went, 'Oh, I've got a bottle of Jack Daniels here.' And Noel goes into the kitchen and he pours it. I walked in and said, 'That's a fucking weird colour,' and he goes to take it – and it's fucking cold tea. My dad is that worried right that when he goes home that I'm going to can the fucking Jack Daniels. He's poured it and pumped it full of fucking cold tea.

PH: SO WHEN DID THE RELATIONSHIP BETWEEN YOU AND OASIS COOL DOWN?

AM: Bit by bit during '95. I was there but I wasn't hands-on at the record company.

PH: There's people saying that you were walking in but you were walking in a daze.

AM: I wasn't there. To be honest, as far as Noel Gallagher was concerned, I had my place on their team for as long as I ever wanted because I'd found them. But I think in '95, I was still trying to get around the question: did I really want to be in the music business? Even though there were still amazing moments. Bits like I'd meet him in Baker Street and he'd go, 'I've done some tracks last week, go and get a tape off Marcus.' And I'd go and get a tape off Marcus and you put it on and it would be 'Wonderwall'. And I told you about that night recently when I played *Morning Glory* just to prove myself right. They fucking were a genius band. That album is just genius. Anyway, there were moments like that. And of course *Morning Glory* came out and we sold ten million albums. But to be honest with you, in my head by now I was saying: do I want to be in the music business? Even as I was standing at Earls Court – the first two Earls Courts were amazing – I was still asking myself that. It wasn't anything to do with success. I was reading about myself in *Music Week* at the end of the year and they would have like Best Marketing Person and Best A&R Person and all these bullshit things. I was the person that the entire music business wanted to have on their team. As much as they went off me by the end of the '90s, in the mid-'90s they all wanted me in their fucking team. And this was at the height of Brit Pop and we absolutely ruled Brit Pop. We had Oasis, Teenage Fanclub and the Boo Radleys. But really deep down kind of going to myself, 'I don't even really know if I want to be here.' And it wasn't until the Maine Road gig that the cloud lifted. I think there were a couple of reasons for that. The first reason was that I got a lot of confidence out of, believe it or not, going up to Manchester and going to the gig. Every time I used to leave London I used to feel really weird. And it was like I was starting to get stronger, mentally. And then the other thing was like working really directly on Ed's album because he was my mate.

PH: WHAT ALBUM IS THAT, WHAT IS IT CALLED?

AM: *Catholic Guilt.* That record started me thinking that I should be in music. I think it's a lovely record and there's some good tunes in it but it was for the love of music. I was working with my friend and that fired me up. So the irony was there I was at 14 million *Morning Glory* sales, but the record that actually made me want to carry on and do music was a record that sold 10,000 copies! But for me it got me back into being involved properly. Emotionally involved. Not just turning up at the meetings and going, 'Yeah, whatever'.

PH: HOW MUCH DID YOU HAVE TO DO WITH *BE HERE NOW*? WERE YOU INVOLVED WITH THAT?

AM: With *Morning Glory* I went down the studio and Liam put on a one man show for me and Dick. It was just unbelievable rants for about an hour. And then the brothers started having an argument and Liam was pinging fucking potatoes off Noel's head and all this sort of stuff. And you could see Noel nearly fucking breaking but not breaking and then him turning round to me and going, 'What about the album? Six out of ten? Seven out of ten?' And then with *Be Here Now* he played us the demos, which was about May 1996, when I was having the time of my life hanging with Ed and starting to enjoy the success of Oasis right. And I remember Noel had me, Dick, Emma Greengrass and Johnny Hopkins round to his gaff.

He played us the demos to *Be Here Now* and I remember thinking, this is gonna sell about half the amount of copies of *Morning Glory*. It's a really intense record. No obvious big hit singles like the other record. But at the end of the day, who was gonna put their hand up and say, 'Noel I think you should maybe shorten most of the songs and not repeat "It's getting better man" 47 times.' Because to be honest, number one, he hadn't been wrong yet. He'd been right. Everything the kid had ever fucking said was right. Number two, even if you were right which basically we all were in our heads, I don't think anybody in that room thought any different from me, which was, this is a guy who has just sold 14 million records and just collected a 15 million pound publishing cheque. Is he actually gonna listen to the bosses in the record company? Was he fuck. So he'd just come back from holiday with Johnny Depp and Kate Moss. He'd sold 15 million records. He'd just banked 15 million pounds. He was living in another dimension by that point.

He made *Be Here Now*. I think it must have been difficult for him because, you know, he got the most amazing reviews in the world ever because the press were absolutely shit scared of Oasis. But at the end of the day nobody was really telling him the truth. And then the fans ultimately told him the truth when it sold six or seven million records which is still loads but half of *Morning Glory*. I mean people went, 'The production is not very good and the songs are a bit low,' and that was the bottom line of it. If Owen [Morris, producer] had been more on it and the songs had been shorter, I think it could have been a really, really great record. My involvement with *Standing On The Shoulder Of Giants*? To be honest they went off to France and there was no invite at all. It was just 'Well, let them get on with it.' To be fair I had the demos and 'Go Let It Out' was the best song on the demos and the rest of the songs were alright but not good enough to be on the record. He did some more demos. He did 'Gas Panic!' and 'Roll It Over' on that bunch. Then he went away to France. At the demo stage we had a bit of input then after that there was no input at all. And he went off to do his thing.

Then he went down to Olympia and he called us all down to play us the single. It was kind of difficult for me that time because it was like, it was proving a point, whether it was Ignition, the management, proving a point or whether it was Noel himself, I don't know. I suspect it was probably Ignition. But the point that was being made was this: McGee, you're on the same level as the Belgian licensee mate because there's Mark Chung over there, there's the guy from 3MV, there's the Belgian licensee, and there's Alan McGee. And I just thought, 'Creatively I have absolutely nothing to do with this band any more because if ever there was a message getting sent out by somebody, I've received the message.' I think that was the next stage of me leaving Creation. It was not a very hard decision for me to make at that point. Because the Primals are self-perpetuating and when the media started saying, 'You're never gonna get another moment as good as Oasis,' they were probably right. And this was at a time when my second most favourite group in the world, behind The Clash, had designated me as important as the fucking Belgian licensee. So the bottom line was, I thought, 'Fuck this for a game of soldiers!'

ED BALL

ED BALL: The Kevin Rowland project, I think, has got to be one of his top four or five projects that he'd ever want to do. And I do think he was shocked at certain points. I mean when Kevin revealed his image he was shocked. I wasn't so shocked. It didn't seem shocking to me. I mean 30 years ago Bowie wore a dress. Reading that book, *The Sharper Word*, talking about John Stephens, men should be comfortable in what they wear. It's almost inevitable that dresses are going to be cutting edge and the furore that was caused is an interesting indictment of that whole generation of people. I dunno, you'll have to ask Alan.

ALAN McGEE

ALAN McGEE: Well, if Paul Weller had been available or Neil Young had been available I'd have signed them. I actually tried to sign Paul Weller. I had John [Weller's manager] in the office and we spoke about it. I put a considerable amount of money on the table and I still never got a meeting. In retrospect, it's probably proper that I never did because if I'd ended up being his enemy or something it would have been a nightmare. Kevin Rowland, I signed him and he's one of my fucking heroes. That's why I signed him. There was £8 million kicking about and it was either going to the tax man or it was getting spent. And I just thought, 'Well I tell you something right, I'd rather give it to Kevin Rowland than the fucking Tories.'

PH: DID YOU SPEND A LOT OF MONEY ON THAT ALBUM?
AM: Yeah. About £270,000 or something like that. But it was quite funny. It was a classic moment right. It's when he showed me the image right. I ran into him in '91 and he was off his fucking tits and I was off my tits. And it's the first time I'd ever seen Kevin Rowland and it was at a Primal Scream afterparty I just went up to him and went, 'I just want to say, fucking double respect man, you were one of the most important guys in fucking pop music. You inspired me to start the label. I'm Alan McGee. Creation.' And he went, 'Alright. I know about you.'

It was brief as fuck. I think the Primals had a couple of parties with him. And this is when he was a fucking real proper fucking charlie head. And like I think he was on a mad cocaine rant about how he'd never want to be part of Creation and all that sort of stuff. That really hurt me right.

You always take criticism from your heroes double bad. But also I was a bit offended by it because I felt, fuck man, you don't know me, Kevin, to say that. I mean being on our label might be good for you or whatever.

Anyway Kevin came out of his *thing* around the same time as me. And he went through a mad one. He was in cults. He was fucking bankrupt. He was like fucking homeless almost. Kevin Rowland was fucking everything that you don't want to be at a certain point in your life. I think he'd got fucked by the whole music industry and fame and drugs. About six or nine months later I got a phone call. Rowland wanted to come and see me. I opened the door and he shows up dressed up as King Henry VIII. Without the crown. Fucking weird socks, velvet trousers and the biggest fur coat ever. But the shoes were Victorian. Bonkers clothes. Now I'm about the only person in the world who is probably going to sign him. He'd be offended by that but I think, at that point, it's probably the truth. The music business *en masse* were scared of Kevin.

So he comes on in and he plays me his demos and he plays two or three tunes and then he gets to this song 'Manhood'.

It's a fucking tune and he takes the fur coat off and he says, 'It's my manhood and this is my manhood' and he sings it. At that point I'm just saying, 'It does not get any fucking better. The greatest fucking singer man. He is the fucking don.' And he's singing his song and I'm just thinking, 'This is why I done it man. This is why I fucking started the record company. To sign Kevin Rowland or Paul Weller or Neil Young or fucking whoever I love.' And at that point I just went, 'You're signed.' And he went, 'I'm signed?'

So we signed him. And it was expensive. It was a six-figure sum. For both albums and we never even ended up getting the second album. Then six months into making the album I pissed him off and he ended up going on holiday because I'd got to him so badly. I was only being me. I was only being honest.

PH: HOW DID YOU PISS HIM OFF?
AM: It's a bit personal. I can't tell you because it's not fair on him but I'd

pissed him off and he ended up biting my head off. I was trying to give him a bit of advice and he didn't want my advice, so it ended up with him getting so stressed out that he went on holiday. And at that point I said to Mark Bowen [Rowland's AR man], 'You'd better try and do it now because I think I'm annoying him. I don't think we're gonna continue the album if I continue doing it.'

Kevin seemed to be sacking an orchestra every week or sacking the fucking session musicians or sacking somebody. It was the highest turnover of fucking musicians and studios. And we did everything on the cheap and it still came in at £270,000. So anyway I stand or fall by this record. People say to me that Creation was a failure at the end of the day, with somebody like Kevin Rowland, because I had to bail him out. Commercially, we lost money doing that record. But from where I'm sitting in the world, I was part of a Kevin Rowland record and it's a work of genius. It's a work of a guy trying to say something: it is probably not the most commercial attempt but the record inside is a piece of genius. It's a beautiful record. So for me that record is a success.

The classic moment of all moments was when he showed me the sleeve. I looked at it – it's Kevin in a skirt in stockings and white pants with make-up on. And I said, 'Fucking hell man, bi-sexual or what!' You cannot change Noel Gallagher's mind. And you cannot change Paul Weller's mind. You cannot change Kevin Rowland's mind. So put out the record. It split the record company in half. Here was one record that ended up fucking splitting the record company in half. Emma Greengrass said it was absolutely disgusting.

PH: HOW DO YOU RESPOND TO THE CRITICISM THAT YOU LET THE IMAGE OVERTAKE THE MUSIC?
AM: Well the thing is, when you get a sleeve like that there's no fucking way that it's not gonna overpower the music. Some people thought that I'd put him up to it. Nick Heyward thought I'd put him up to it. He said to Ed, 'How did Alan get Kevin to do that?' You don't get Kevin Rowland to do anything. That's the point of Kevin Rowland.

He's genius, man. I would like to hope that me and Kevin are cool and sweet with each other because I think an awful lot of Kevin. He's probably one of the biggest characters I have ever had on my label.

PH: THERE WAS ANOTHER THING YOU SAID LAST TIME. ANOTHER ALBUM THAT YOU REALLY ENJOYED MAKING AT THIS PERIOD WAS TRASHMONK'S *MONA LISA OVERDRIVE*.

AM: Making the Trash Monk record was also one of the moments. Ed and I were running this Living Room. I'd just come out of rehab. And Ed was saying, 'Right, we're gonna get you back right in the music. We're gonna get you back in the business. Bang into it.' I cheekily replied, 'Oh how are you gonna do that then? Are you gonna give me an injection?' But just he went, 'No. I'm gonna fucking start a club with you. We're gonna do an acoustic club. I'll play. And we'll get all our mates to play.'

PH: Was this his intent. 'Here you are Alan, remember your roots'?

AM: Yeah, yeah. That was Ed's way of saying, 'You're going to fucking pull it together.'

PH: HE'S A GOOD FRIEND TO YOU ISN'T HE?

AM: He's brilliant. He's one of my best friends. So we've got this club. And I was deejaying and this lunatic kid came upstairs. Except he's 38, this guy. He comes up and he goes, 'Hello, I'm Nick. I used to be in Dream Academy'. I said, 'You've one really great song.' 'What's that?' he enquired. '"Love Parade",' I goes, 'My first wife cleared the house out and left me to the sound of "Love Parade". I kept putting your 12-inch on as she was clearing out half my record collection.' He was laughing. So then and he says, 'Can I come and play you songs?' He came and played me old Dream Academy demos, right, and it was all fucking '80s stuff.

I said, 'I'm not being funny mate but to be absolutely honest music's moved on.' He went, 'Well it's funny you should say that: I've done this one thing,' he goes, 'I don't know if it's good or not.' And he put it on. I went, 'It's fucking amazing. That is fucking amazing. That's what you should fucking do.'

PH: WHAT YEAR IS THIS?

AM: Christmas '95. He spent the next three years making the album. He's been through what I've been through. He's made loads of money. He's went up a mountain. He's lost the plot completely. He's had a nervous breakdown. Ended up in a fucking Buddhist retreat for nine months. Got his shit back.

By default, I end up being the A&R man. It was brilliant fun. I'd go down there every six weeks. And then we got into the mixing process. That's when it really became fun and worth every day. He made me remember who I really was.

We did this press release and he's such an obsessive lunatic that he made about 80 changes in red ink. And then I made something like about 20 changes. And we put the three bits of paper down. And it just looked the most mental thing ever. And I went, 'That's the fucking press release.' And he went, 'It can't be the press release, it's unreadable.' We sent it out and people like Roy Carr were sending it back saying, 'Sorry but you sent us the original.' 'No mate, that *is* the press release.' It was old school Creation. Creation for the right reasons. Creation because it's a fucking top record and because it's not trying to sell a million records. We don't even release a single off it. We just put it out. And it sold about 40,000 copies round the world.

PH: Ed Ball said 'I never worried about him during his drug days. I got worried when I heard Alan saying things like, "Some Sony guy I went out with".'

AM: I think you get caught up in that environment.

PH: But you told me the music biz hates you.

AM: They do.

PH: SO DID YOU PISS THE MUSIC BUSINESS OFF DELIBERATELY?

AM: I don't think I deliberately pissed them off but I did piss them off by default. I got inside the machine. I didn't even mean to do it. I genuinely didn't mean to get inside the machine. But I did it because I'm a Labour Party supporter. I joined the Labour Party when I cleaned up. Somebody looked down the Labour Party register and saw Alan

McGee, Bickenhall Street. So they gave me a phone call. Derek Draper gave me a phone call. And he was working for the Labour Party and Peter Mandelson at the time.

He sussed out that I was Alan McGee and he said, 'Do you think Oasis would do something for us?' He brought along the General Secretary of the Labour Party, Margaret McDonagh. Suddenly in the course of one conversation I went from being a guy they hadn't even bothered returning a membership card to being a major player in the Labour Party. It was very weird. Suddenly saying to me, 'Can you organise something for the Labour Party Conference? Matthew Freud and Lord Waheed Ali are putting the money up for it. We've got Cream DJs.'

I phoned up Marcus and Noel. Marcus said, 'I tell you what: why don't we just give them a Platinum disc?' We got 18 Wheeler and Ed to do this Labour Party do. And Blair walks in with Cherie and suddenly we're getting our picture taken and Ed's got his picture taken. So then I got up on stage and I give Tony the fucking Platinum disc.

You've got to understand, I hate the Conservatives. And me and Dick have just bagged 14-and-a-half million right out of Sony and the next thing is we're hanging with the main people of the Labour Party. One night Kate and I were talking about giving money to the Scottish Labour Party – because Scotland's the place that's been fucked over. I give the Labour Party £50,000 and it ends up on the front page of the *Scottish Daily Record*. It became one of my greatest ever moments. Not only because it was the front page but it was three pages of me ranting about how much I hate Tories. So the bottom line is, Labour win. I just think that's it. I swear to you if they gave me a Sir Alan McGee OBE, MBE or CBE I'd tell them to stick it up their fucking arse. I hate the Royal Family. I hate the Conservatives. I don't want any fucking honours from the fucking Establishment.

I've got one O Level and I don't give a fuck. The reason I gave that money was to get the Tories out of Scotland because they fucking raped and pillaged Scotland. That's what the money was given for. So I get a phone call first of all from Geoffrey Robinson the Paymaster General.

He says, 'We want to use you as the figurehead to get young Britain back to work.' And I replied, 'I hate to tell you this mate but the people I sell records to don't, generally speaking, want to have a job. And if I'm seen to be putting them back to work I think my record sales and my bands might fucking drop in half so I'm gonna have to decline.'

So what *do* I want? I want musicians to not be on the dole and to get paid for being a musician. So I start this campaign. And it's called New Deal for Musicians. So I start doing it. And the whole of the music business are anti me doing it. Why should it be hard for people? Why don't we help people instead of making it hard for people? I mean give people a chance. The people that are successful don't neccessarily have to have it hard. That's bollocks. You can have talent but if you get defeated too many times – I'm thinking of working-class people – it can fucking destroy you, so why don't we try and grow instead of fucking slaughter it?

The second thing I did that really fucking upset them was this article about the Internet and *NME*. And I predicted that there would be mergers with Internet companies who would buy the music business companies – people would lose their jobs and bands would lose their record deals. The Internet is a way forward for people. Ultimately music would be cheaper but more people would consume. Talk about fucking nuking the music industry. Man alive. I have never known such fucking vitriol come my way. I went from being like 'loveable outsider, extremely successful maverick person' to bogeyman overnight.

I don't mind Rob Dickens and all these people having a pop at me because they're right-wing and I'm left-wing and it will always be that way. On an intellectual level I actually got on well with him. He's a lot cleverer than me in a lot of ways but I think I'm a lot more instinctive than he is about music. I think we've both ultimately probably got some degree of respect for each other. What pissed me off was people like Tony Wilson and the guy that found Joy Division who are just corporate whores now sucking up to the music industry. And then ironically, two years later, Tony Wilson's in charge of two or three websites and trying to sell people music! It's like: 'You don't even believe in what you're saying an more, Tony. I mean, fucking hell, have a look in the mirror. It's fucking ugly. But we're all looking at it.

CHAPTER SEVEN

JOE FOSTER: The Primals were a supreme band. They've been there the whole time and through it all. They were the ones that carried through the whole attitude, the whole love of music and love of all different kinds of things. They're totally eclectic. And that's what Creation were always about.

LAURENCE: I think that Creation is probably the most inspirational label that exists. Look at Primal Scream. 'Loaded' was one of the most interesting, cutting edge, melting-pot kind of records that took Acid House and rock 'n' roll culture into one thing. I still think My Bloody Valentine is one of the most amazing bands as well. We don't have the distance to appreciate all this stuff to its fullest extent, but when you look at the Peel session of the Mary Chain, which has been released recently, when was the last time pop music had something like that? I don't think a lot of new labels have got that heavyweight talent. Majors are about profit, about product and getting it consumed. Creation was people learning about music and loving it.

I'm glad Alan is going back to the woods. He is still very curious about music. He got into drum 'n' bass at one point. I'm really proud of Creation. I think that it is so good that he has left them. I think it is good, because there is nothing like that anymore, is there?

KLE: Those were the good old days and I don't think I'm glamorising it. I think they really were the good old days. Don't get me wrong. At the time there were days when I'd go home in tears, but there was life in it then; there was a passsion and everyone stuck around because it was where they wanted to be. I'm not bitter about the way things started to wind down. That's life and life is change and no matter how great or how bad something is, it's just never going to last. I'm so thankful that I was there for the good times.

LAURENCE: Alan finishing Creation didn't come as a surprise to me. I knew why Alan did Creation; I knew why he loved it. Alan loves music.

SIMON STEPHENS: When I met McGee last time he'd seen me with my little boy of three months on Primrose Hill and he said, 'I saw you walking down Primrose Hill and I turned round to Innes and said is that his kid or has he nicked it?' To think that you would go and nick a kid and walk around Primrose Hill! But there you go, that's fucking Alan. He has got a mind and a half on him, he does. We had some fucking funny times. He was always preoccupied with business.

ED BALL: The reason why we all love the guy is because he's the record company boss we'd all love to be. I tried and failed. I threw down the gauntlet and said, 'You're the fucking man and I want to join the team.' I think that's what it is. That's the difference between him and the bloke that runs Sony. The man who runs Sony could be selling Daz washing powder. It wouldn't make a difference.

JF: Any of the bands on Creation were really quite interesting people. It kind of drifted away from having exceptional people. We had our moments. But in general, it is a *true* picture: we did hang out, we did all like each other, we were all part of each other's lives and all the rest of it. That was part of the success of it. You'd be in each other's pockets all the time and you'd get whacky ideas from people.

EB: I see Creation Records as one of the few things that got us through the '80s and is now only starting to be understood. I think what Alan McGee brought to the table was hope for people who wanted to make music, who wanted to start a label, who wanted to do something. It was a maverick label. It was very much like Apple in that anyone could come along and could talk a crazy idea, and Alan would be into it, half for the cheek of it all. Drug damage? There's a few things I notice in myself that I've lost. Apart from my hair. Thought processes sometimes are a bit bemused. But by and large I think we came through alright. Everybody pulled their socks up. Everybody had a good time. I think we all pulled through.

SUSAN McGEE

SUSAN McGEE: I never went to Knebworth. I went to Loch Lomond but the whole Oasis phenomenon was just unbelievable. I mean, it was mental. We were getting a chauffeur-driven car to Loch Lomond and back. And I took my friend who lived in this council estate in Possil, which is one of the worst places in Glasgow. I deliberately picked her up because it was chauffeur-driven. Everybody was waving at her and it was like the Gala Day or something in Possil. They were all waving and saying 'There's a Limo coming in the area!' And then we drove off while everybody was waving. That was good.

ALAN McGEE

ALAN McGEE: Because of the way I grew up, my life expectation was nil right? I was the one that was born without good looks. I was a write-off. Everybody wrote me off. Not even my mum and dad thought I was ever gonna fucking do anything. So when your parents don't even believe in you right, the bottom line is, you don't even believe in yourself. But I believed in Dexy's Midnight Runners, The Jam, The Sex Pistols, The Clash and Punk rock.

I wanted to be part of that. I'd no expectations. I thought I was in the factory for the rest of my life. So when I started doing music and started managing the Mary Chain my parents started noticing me again. I was always doing it for my mum really. In '84 my parents started noticing me and blaming Laura which was shit for her. I was doing it to say to my mum, 'I'm actually a good person. I've actually got some talent. I'm not academically bright. I'm not good looking, I'm not going to go out with Kate Moss. I'm not the best fighter in the street. But I'm good at finding bands and they pay me money for it. And now I can send you away off on holiday.' I know it sounds pathetic but my mum's expectation was zero. So by the time it all fucking rolled out and by the time it kind of got to '94 I was in another world. But what was driving me, what I was trying to say to my mum was: I am alright.

A CREATION SELECTION

ALAN McGEE TOP TWELVE

Xtrmntr – Primal Scream

Screamadelica – Primal Scream

Isn't Anything – My Bloody Valentine

Loveless – My Bloody Valentine

Definitely Maybe – Oasis

What's The Story (Morning Glory) – Oasis

Mona Lisa Overdrive – Trash Monk

Giant Steps – Boo Radleys

My Beauty – Kevin Rowland

Bandwagonesque – Teenage Fan Club

House Of Love – House Of Love

The Man – Bill Drummond

ED BALL TOP TEN

Loveless – My Bloody Valentine

Love Is Forever – Biff Bang Pow

Echo Dek – Primal Scream

Xtrmntr – Primal Scream

Definitely Maybe – Oasis

Keeping The Faith – Vols 1 and 2

Pied Piper Of Feedback – Slaughter Joe

Forever Breathes The Lonely Word – Felt

House Of Love – House Of Love

Threads – Dave Kinsworth and the
——————Bounty Hunters

JOE FOSTER

Personally I like all the Primals albums, all the Valentines albums. Tony Barber would say the first Jasmine Minks album and I'd put it in there on his behalf. I don't know, basically they're all great. If we hadn't thought all these people were brilliant we would never have made records with them.

ALAN McGEE AND THE STORY OF CREATION RECORDS